Pomba Gira
and the Quimbanda of Mbùmba Nzila

Nicholaj de Mattos Frisvold

Pomba Gira
and the Quimbanda of Mbùmba Nzila

SCARLET IMPRINT · MMXI

Published by Scarlet Imprint
© Nicholaj de Mattos Frisvold, 2011
Edited by Peter Grey & Alkistis Dimech
Design & *pontos riscados* by Alkistis Dimech
Pomba Gira illustrations by Enoque Zedro

ISBN 978-0-9567203-7-5

SCARLETIMPRINT.COM

Contents

Illustrations

Acknowledgments

This book is dedicated to Woman in all
her forms & manifestations. I will also give
tribute to Iya Eyebomi Adetutu, my constant
partner in life, love and mystery, who always
deserves praise for her love, support and
patience in all of life's beautiful mysteries.
Gratitude is also due to Adriano Draconis,
always steady medium, brother and priest and
Jesse Hathaway, loyal brother in the many
ways of the Art. Roy Kirkland should also be
given recognition for questions that lead to
some of his suggestions finding their way into
this tome. Thanks is also due to Diego de Exu,
Anderson (Nehaher), Oliver Seymour, Luiza
Pastor and Mario Chimanovitch for their
presence in the world.

And lastly, may great blessings be cast upon
Peter and Alkistis for being who they are,
beautiful rebels in a mesmerising world of
riddles!

Disclaimer

This book contains herbal formulæ of spell-craft that must be viewed as being of interest only for the anthropologist, ethnobotanist & researchers in general. Neither the author nor the publisher endorse the use of these herbal substances in any way, juvenile or cunning as they may be. We refrain from any responsibility given upon us by anyone who has, in a learned or immature way, attempted to apply potentially poisonous and dangerous formulæ in their life upon reading this book. As such, those parts of the book should be viewed as curiosities of the cult.

*The goddess fierce Echidna
who is half a nymph with
glancing eyes and fair cheeks,
and half again a huge snake,
great and awful, with speckled
skin, eating raw flesh beneath
the secret parts of the holy
earth. And there she has a cave
deep down under a hollow rock
far from the deathless gods and
mortal men. There, then, did
the gods appoint her a glorious
house to dwell in: and she keeps
guard in Arima beneath the
earth, grim Echidna, a nymph
who dies not nor grows old all
her days.*

Herodotus,
Theogony 295–305

P OMBA GIRA is a living and ever evolving vibrant enigma. She has been subject to a multitude of interpretations which all speak of her ability to shed her skin and show herself in an astonishing array of manifestations, just as Venus herself does. She is a garden of erotic strength that inspires awe for women and provokes humility in men. No man working with these forces can escape being intrigued and humbled by the greatness and diversity of woman in all her manifestations.

When I wrote the book *Kiumbanda*, published in 2006, it was initially met with harsh resistance in Brazil, and one French researcher deemed that I had created a new form of Quimbanda. It suffered an even harsher critique which discarded my work as unrelated to Quimbanda in any way. All this, in spite of using solely the material of practitioners who defined this cult more than half a decade ago. *Kiumbanda* was an attempt to rescue a vast amount of knowledge that was about to enter oblivion. After a couple of years the resistance gave way to acceptance and I realised that the element of provocation rested in the fact that my now deceased teacher had tutored me in what is called *kimbanda de raiz*, or kimbanda from the root, considered to be a more original form of the cult. It is probably from this that we find the quite common idea that Quimbanda (with a *q*) is more spiritually pure than Kimbanda (with a *k*). In the course of the antagonism I became gradually aware that I had not created anything new, but rather I had been blessed with a traditional insight into the world of Quimbanda that gave proper tribute to the legacy of its masters.

In this book I have decided to take matters much further than I did in *Kiumbanda*, which was merely a presentation of the cult. My perspective on the cult has matured and I also feel more free in imparting the wisdom which the spirits have given to me, along with good counsel and orientation from other priests and priestesses of the cult. I have come to realise the essentially skin-shedding nature of this terrible and mesmerising power as she unveils herself across cultures, time and geography.

Over the years I have visited many centers and temples of worship and spoken with countless practitioners. What is common is that Pomba Gira intrigues people; there is a magnetic pull at work. I have seen people falling prey to her challenges as much as I have seen people reaching wonderful states of maturity and enlightenment. She is complex and she is a spirit – or a legion called deity if you will – that constantly provokes and challenges us. This can be through domination, seduction or bewilderment. I have found that she always seeks to temper and challenge the belief and self-image of people who approach her in order to shake them free from falsity and reveal the raw truth.

Quite commonly she is viewed as the experienced woman of the streets and lower class, sometimes as a forfeited aristocratic concubine and scorned mistress. It is this wisdom of being human and learning how to ascend which I feel is important for them to teach us. Here you walk through the crossroad and it becomes the cross and the road, ever turning and changing.

The contents of this book are an honest presentation of the wisdom communicated to me by good people (and some bad people) as well as my own connection with Pomba Gira developed over some fifteen years. The intention is to make this intriguing cult accessible and understandable in a way that enables people of all walks of life and cultures to glimpse her.

I will continue to honor the teachings of my mentors and this includes those I never met, but who influenced my teachers, like Aluizio Fontenelle, Antônio Alves Teixeira and N.A. Molina. And I evoke my past masters when I say as they did, that this book is indeed the truth I found under the embrace of spirit and men and women blessed by spirit. I hope this wisdom given so generously to me by spirit will benefit you and add positively to the understanding of the mysterious, wonderful and enigmatic Pomba Gira. As she is without shame, I too give shamelessly this grammar and testament to the world, this vision upon tradition; I leave the zealots to their own devices!

Tata Sigatana
Cabula Mavambo Ngobodi Nzila *xiii*

UIMBANDA is largely understood as a *black art* because it is here that we find the cult of the devil and his wife. The red world of the devil's spouse and mistress merges into his darkness as roaring laughter bursts from the pits of hell and mischievous acts are incessantly performed. One petitions the aid of the powers of Quimbanda whether one seeks to tie another's heart in a desperate obsession, or if seeking the insanity or downfall of an adversary. It is said that Exu and Pomba Gira work fast and will give, bound by contract, whatever vulgar or worldly desire you might seek to attain. Quimbanda seizes its potency in the great hour, midnight itself, where Venus Vespertina oversees the secret rites of riot, revolt, hatred and lust. By candle, blood, spirit signature, prayer and song, these denizens of hell are brought forth to provide solace. Their fierce reputation often distorts the simple message they convey — namely that they reflect your passions, and that hell is already here. The majority of people seeking the aid of Exu and Pomba Gira are in despair and torment — they are experiencing their own hell and as a result they are already in the realm of Exu and Pomba Gira. What in time became known as Quimbanda was in the past referred to as *macumba* or simply black magic; the diabolic imagery was a constant theme, so it is only natural that they came to accept and absorb the diabolic iconography attributed to them. It is important to understand that Quimbanda is part of a complex and breathtaking socio-magical skin-shedding activity. Macumba was the tool used by *the people of the streets*, the outcasts, slaves, free-born slaves and all strata of society that suffered under oppression. The diabolical realm was seen as inhabited by spirits not weighed down by morality and ethics. They did not judge, but instead they understood, and on the basis of this mutual understanding pacts were made. The intention in the past was not to go to a spirit, ask a favor, make the contract and then leave the pact upon completion, as is common today. Our dealings with spirits are often plagued with the faulty ideals of consumerism. The spirit retinue of Quimbanda has much to give and can aid in maturing our understanding of the world, if we can only allow them to do so. Doing this invites challenges, for to take on the devil as one's tutor will not make for a safe journey. They are hard and demanding teachers that at times perplex in their responses and actions as they seek work to heal the tormented human soul. This ultimately provides greater solace than the quick fix of a problem that will simply recur unless we come to understand its root causes. When faced with obsession, despair, passion – all matters of the heart – Pomba Gira is the one who knows intimately the essence of these afflictions and how these matters can be solved in a compact of understanding. It is here we find the avenue where a geographically located cult, like Quimbanda, has global value. To make this avenue more viable and visible it is important to venture deeper down the twain and twisted roots of Quimbanda.

The Nocturnal Roots of Forgetfulness

Quimbanda is a word derived from the Kimbundu-speaking people in the upper parts of the district of Mbundu in Angola, *ki'mbanda* being the plural form of medium. We find the same origin in the word

Umbanda which is derived from *mbanda*, the singular form of medium amongst the Kimbundu and Mbundu-speaking people of Angola. The idea of being a medium is more broad in scope than someone who simply receives spirit communications. Amongst the cults of diviners and healers, like the Nkita and Ngombe cults in the vast region of Congo and Angola, mediumship was of a more prophetic nature. A kimbanda was someone who was seen as having a unique connection with Nzambi and through this would convey messages of truth, healing and restoration for individuals and society. The role might have been more similar to that of the shaman who is divinely appointed to take care of the spiritual well-being of his people. This indicates that the medium would possess remedies for healing, protection and combat in his arsenal. The wider connotation of the world of the mbanda is today largely forgotten in favor of the image of the *quimbandeiro* being more akin to the iconic amoral sorcerer.

We find this connotation attached to Quimbanda through its earlier names Macumba and Magia Negra (Black Magic). Macumba was not a term restricted to the cult of Exu and Pomba Gira, but was used as a generic signifier for any form of nocturnal magical practice. The word Macumba is most likely from the Kikongo *mayumba* which means *a magical working that ignites insanity*. As we can see, there is a strong Congo legacy at work in the cult of Quimbanda that was reinforced dramatically in the 70s with the simultaneous decline of the conception of a non-African ancestry for Quimbanda. From this afrocentric reclaiming, reconstructions of various forms took place, most notably the adoption of Exu and Pomba Gira into many houses of Candomblé. Here we find the origin of the contemporary diffusion and confusion between Exu, the diabolic force in Quimbanda and the Orixa Èsú. Ngola, Kikongo and Kimbundu words were also adopted into the cult, leading both to a more concise liturgy, but also a distortion of African ideas by understanding several key concepts on Western premises. All this led to a greater diversity in Quimbanda and Umbanda. For instance, recently the concept of *nkulu* has been taking shape amongst quimbandeiros. This describes the essentially nocturnal nature of Exu and Pomba Gira as malevolent spirits. In its Kimbundu origin, nkulu designates the soul, but it also has ancestral inferences. It may or may not be used to describe an ancestor of malevolent orientation. There are also the kabalistic forms of Quimbanda as well as the spiritualist, satanic and ceremonial forms. The most curious one is probably the work of Rivas Neto and his cosmic Hindu-Lemurian synthesis based on 'high magic' vaguely rooted in Eliphas Lévi. Confronted by this great variety it is evident that this 'cult of mediums' replicates a diversity similar to that of the healers and mediums in Congo and Angola. The spirits inspire and manifest in varied ways – the only faults in this mediumistic resurgence lie squarely with the medium and the whole complex of possession and doctrine.

Within the cult of Pomba Gira and Exu we are confronted with cultural forgetfulness paired with social need. In this field of necessity and lies, devotion and truth, the spirits dance in man's heart and life. This is natural in a constantly skin-shedding cult and as Roger Bastide comments in his research: *memories inherited from the ancestors survive only insofar as they can insinuate themselves into the existing framework of society* (Bastide 1978: 258). This loss of substance, as he calls it, is the vacuum that spirit fills through mediumistic transmission. Bastide takes a somewhat negative attitude towards this and states that this ancestral forgetfulness is filled with new elements that are extraneous to the African root. This might be so, but I believe matters are more complicated: there is a play between the recognition of the old in new designs, and a recourse to modern elements to replace the lost fragments. Thus, Quimbanda moves and pirouettes and replicates the essential nature of the Craft of the Wise in its fluid flux across time. If we acknowledge this proposition to be useful in understanding the complexity of Quimbanda, it can provide an explanation as to why we find such diversity both in the performance of the cult and the various expressions of the cult ranging from the diabolic to the more speculative New Age forms. In spite of its constantly evolving nature, the fundamental premises of the cult are always in place and at the centre stands the medium as the pillar for the spirit's ascent and descent.

Given such diversity, the roots of Quimbanda have been subject to great dispute, both between scholars and practitioners. These disagreements have at times led to stasis. This is quite evident in one of the few studies on Brazilian cults and religiosity in the English language by Diana D. Brown (*Umbanda*, 1986) where she gives up and resorts to guesswork of an ill-informed nature. This shows the complexity and difficulty in understanding how both Umbanda and Quimbanda came to be what they are today. The sociologist, historian and painter Gilberto Freyre commented in 1933 that it was perhaps best to see the religious developments in Brazil as less religious and more social. By this he meant that social need was the prime factor that provoked change, interaction and stability from centre to centre across Brazil. In a recent study, professor of music Marc Gidal rekindles our memory by reminding us how Quimbanda was worked prior to the social changes in Brazil in the 70s. Gidal points out how, as late as in the 50s, one could go to a centre or terreiro of Umbanda and witness the limited attention given to Exu and Pomba Gira. Commonly, a ceremony consisting of minutes in honor to the owners of the great hour (midnight) was performed. The ceremony was restricted to a petition, and possessions, if they happened at all, were described as brutal and wild with the mediums growling and shouting in the most nefarious manifestations. Today, Pomba Gira and Exu come down in more civilised ways and give counsel, help with spells, and give advice – a position originally pertaining to the *preto velhos*, or ol' Blacks, seen as the omnipresent ancestral wisdom. With the possessions becoming more elaborate, so too did the drum patterns and the amount of *pontos cantados* – the songs that give praise and songs which invite possession and manifestation. Quimbanda has become the cult of the common people. Everyone can come to Pomba Gira when their heart is broken, in suffering and pain. She never judges, but always understands – because she is you – only many lifetimes wiser. This makes it very difficult to judge various forms of Quimbanda as more legitimate than others – in the end it is up to the quality of the mediums to relay wisdom inspired by spirit that can work upon us in a positive way.

The nature of possession invites the question of how reliable the transmission is. In many instances I have witnessed possessions that are not so much spirit manifesting as they are an exercise of the psyche. This means that one is exercising parts of the self which are denied or suppressed in daily life. Possession then takes on the function of catharsis, or a lower exercise of the form of the spirit called upon. This can often lead to purification in its own right where one's demons are exorcised and pacified. These possessions do not necessarily provide any spiritual insight, but should still be acknowledged for their positive effects, that is, if we are honest about what is going on. Honesty in place, these forms of psychic possession can often be a good thing. The quality of possessions is in my opinion directly dependent on the tronco or the solidity of the house. The more steady and good the tronco is, the more reliable the spirit communication is, and the need for total possession is lessened. When the tronco is good, it appears as if the whole room is saturated in spirit and it is often sufficient to place oneself under the inspiration of this cloud of spiritual fire flowing around the sacred space. A good tronco serves as a steady foundation for the cult that sheds it skin in celebrating each new night upon the earth.

6

This renewal of form, this skin-shedding quality is evident everywhere. Let us take for instance the icon of Pomba Gira Mulambo. In one of her pontos cantados we sing:

Mulambe Mulambe a Mulambe e Nganga

The word *mulambe* appears to be slightly corrupted from its origin, and it is difficult to tell for certain what it actually refers to. It can be a reference to the *mulemba* or African fig tree, a notorious haven for the witches' powers – but it can also be taken from the Kikongo *lambe* which is related to purifications. The ponto quoted is used precisely for purification purposes and is to be sung when one is exorcising spiritual impurities such as obsessive spirits and malevolent elementals. So, we can understand the ponto as speaking of purification being the power of this priest/ess (*nganga*). Mulambo is also jargon for rag, and related to Maria Lixeira, a Pomba Gira that dwells in rotten places, whether sewers, rubbish tips, trash cans or urine-soaked back alleys on hot steamy nights, without herself being tainted. She is the one that oversees the purification because she can take away all impurities without any harm to herself. On one hand we have an African memory connected to her form and function either as a purifier, or as the owner of the fig tree; on the other hand we have the story of Maria Rosa who forfeited a king's marriage proposal in favor of her true love for a poor man. We are told that the poor man manages to make her pregnant, infuriating the barren king who searches after her for seven nights and murders her at the shore of the river. In this story we find themes reminiscent of hagiography, drawn in part from the legends of St. Catharina and St. Luzia. In addition we find sorcerous elements from local fairy tales, in this case the ghost of Maria Rosa comes at night to comfort her one true love. It is quite evident to me that she is all of these, and as such we need to perceive Pomba Gira as a theme that speaks of a particular mystery. Hence, she shines through the diverse ways of worship and reverence, being more than the dogmatic refrains of a given cult. Define her as your property and she will surely dare you and challenge the chains you lay before her. By assuming the figure of the woman of seven husbands she is also assuming her role as a free woman.

Umbanda is intimately connected to Quimbanda and together they share the African roots that are maintained in the class of spirits called *preto velhos* (ol' Blacks). They have names like Pai Congo, Vó Cabinda or common names like Vó Catarina and Pai Cipriano. They are also separated into lineages defined by geographical origin. They can be from Congo, Arruanda, Angola, the Woods and so forth, and are said to work under a line controlled by an Orixa. In addition we have the class of spirits called *caboclos*, or Indians. This is the wisdom of the new land speaking, whereas the old blacks represent ancestry itself. It is in this dynamic field that Umbanda and Quimbanda were shaped, both before and after the founding of Umbanda by Zelio in 1908, after the Caboclo das Sete Encruzilhadas (Caboclo Seven Crossroads) manifested in a séance announcing the birth of a new faith that would bring together people of all classes and orientations. The idea of the mediumistic focus as being derived from Kardec's spiritism is perhaps overstated, as the type of mediumistic work we find in Umbanda is also found amongst the Bantu speaking people from where Umbanda took shape. The focus on Kardec seems to be more a tactical move than anything else. Spiritism had a great appeal for the middle classes and thus, by resorting to European spiritism instead of African mediumship, Umbanda was able to gain a broader appeal. After all, at the root of Umbanda we find forces that aimed towards a unification of Brazilian cults through mediumistic activity. Not only this, but the principles of charity, humility and wisdom important in Kardescism are also associated with the preto velhos.

The relationship between Umbanda and Quimbanda is a strong one; the Umbandistas, between 1908 and 1920, were the ones who actually rescued the practice of Macumba from obscurity. It was a framework that enabled this pragmatic form of sorcery to merge with the land in a way that testifies to its inherent dynamic flame.

It follows that we should perceive the diversity within the cult as its inherent nature. This is due to an astonishing variety of common themes. In many ways I feel the idea of *maqām* as we find in Sufism and Middle Eastern music is a worthy allegory for the nature of the cult. The maqām is a technique of improvisation upon traditional scales that generates a unique expression in terms of both composition and performance. It is also the seven dwellings of the Sufi saint, where restoration and purification occur on the path towards divine union. Each maqām provides teachings and challenges, so we can journey on towards the final station that destiny has appointed for us. This idea is also found in the doctrine, presented by some deceased priests and priestesses, who saw the connection with Pomba Gira undergo a similar development, each stage being a dwelling of teaching ranging from her pagan and wild manifestations to the regal and stable ones. In maqām compositions a similar idea develops, as the composition is not ruled by rhythm and melody but rather by the space between the tones. Mastery of the maqām denotes perfection as the harmonies of the spheres are made manifest. It is from such perspectives, which perhaps seem like alien metaphors, that we can understand the diversity we find in Quimbanda.

The origin of contemporary Quimbanda is like many tributaries flowing into one great river. It follows from this that to define with absolute precision the origins of the cult is not only impossible, but perhaps not the best way to understand the cult. What we know is that present day Quimbanda was a century ago called Macumba and it is in the rites of the macumbeiros we find the crossroad of sorcerous practice, both indigenous, European and African that colours the cult today in so many diverse shades. Macumba used to be a pejorative term for black magic and this in the truest sense of the word, as meaning African sorcery.

The Two Tables

It was in the state of Minas Gerais that Quimbanda took form. From the late 18th century in Minas Gerais we find *quilombos* (martially ordered slave camps). In the state of Espirito Santo the quilombos were called *cabula*. With the abolition of slavery they were dissolved and merged into the greater sphere of Macumba to resurface together with Umbanda. In these quilombos the priests were called nganga and they made cults to Nzampiempungo and Kalunga and Cariacariapemba. Here we find the origin of the *gira*, or *ngira* as a reference to the cabula or brotherhood itself. The Bishop of Espirito Santo, Dom João Nery, who left office in 1901, had a unique insight into the cabula sect which he shared in his pastoral letters to the Holy Office. I find his account most interesting, both in terms of content and because of the few family lines of macumbeiros/cabuleiros that are still in secret existence in Brazil. In these documents we are told that the gathering was held in complete secrecy and all who entered were sworn to silence to avoid the cup of poison that would otherwise be their share. They would call upon the spirits of Tatá, ancestral spirit guides, and today the name given to the office of Kimbanda mastery as well as those teaching Exu. The rituals were organised in a temple, called *camucite*, around two *mesas* (major tables) and other smaller ones. In Nery's account the main tables were dedicated to Santa Barbara and Mary, the Immaculate Virgin. In addition there was a secret table for Saints Cosmas and Damian, the divine twins. The guardians of this table were dressed from head to foot in black, and introduced the essence of the mysteries of the dead. The description of their clothing recalls the *egungun* clothing. Egungun is a Yoruba word that means loosely *bones of ancestry* and represents the collective wisdom of the ancestors. The spirit only comes down when the medium is dressed in the *aso egungun*, the cloth of the egungun. This is a colourful dress that covers the medium from head to foot, no part of the skin is exposed, in memory of how the bones of ancestry were completely covered so that their essence would remain a completely veiled secret. Each table had a magister, called *enbanda*, meaning chief-medium, and was assisted by a *cambone*, a loyal person who would safeguard the medium. With the mediums in possession the cambones lead the barefoot congregation, dressed in white, out to a sacred place in the dark woods. Well placed in the wilderness beneath an appointed sacred tree with tables and statues brought for the occasion, they light a bonfire at the centre of the circle. Seated in the appointed location, a candle ceremony is performed; the first one is lit for Calunga (the spirit of the Ocean) in the east, followed by the other three directions. At this point the head of the enbanda is covered and handkerchiefs are tied around his arms, as we find in Vodou. He calls out to Calunga and Tatá and the *bacúlo* (spirits) to give the *enbanda quendá* – or to give the medium an entrance. The call is accompanied with rhythms and songs until the enbanda is taken over by his Tatá and starts to growl and scream under the pressure of the spirit entering. With the Tatá seated in the enbanda he is given wine and a sacred root, most likely *juremá*. At times he also demands to eat *candarú*, which are the fiery embers from the rich incense burning in front of the tables. The medium then calls to the bacúlo of the air to possess him at the table while he swirls around it (*girar*). From this point playing with fire begins, as the medium enters into the form of his Tatá and embers are given to them 'to speak upon'. The *ninbú* (songs) following from this are all attuned to the number three. There are three Tatás calling him and three *candarás* (initates) calling for him. It is in this state the initiation happens. The camucite (the one presenting the *caiálo* for initiation) now enters and passes through the legs of the enbanda three times to underline the importance of faith, humility and obedience to the Tatá. Cuts are made and *embá* (magical powders) are placed in the cuts. He is then given the sacred root and wine. The embá is then rubbed on the head, front, nape and crowns of the attending people while an oracle is pronounced for the newly initiated. The new initiate is then given a candle that is passed from all sides through the legs of the Tatá and his or her own legs while the candidate is being whipped. This goes on until the flame goes out. The ritual seals the faith of the new member. This accomplished, the congregation engages in *santé*, possession by their saint, guiding spirit or Tatá. For a lapse in time, gods are dancing in the forest.

The good Bishop also tells how one seeks out one's patron, santé or Tatá by taking a candle into the woods where it will be lit under the powers of his Tatá which will then give its name. Curiously, this is an integral part of the Nordic practice of sorcery known as *seidr*: to sit down in a place of power calling out for the spirit to come until you are taken over. The name given can be the real name of the spirit or it can be a generic name as we see in the legions of Quimbanda where an attribute is related to a location in one of the kingdoms.

What is beautiful in this account is how truthful Quimbanda has been to its core. In spite of the great diversity Quimbanda still maintains the essential mediumistic point of ingress under the watchful eyes of the spirit of fire, Cariacariapemba/Lukankazi. It is from this spirit we might trace the origin of Exu in the guise of St. Barbara. Pomba Gira has a different origin, here lodged in the table of Mary, Immaculate Virgin. What is quite stunning is that her Congo and her current name both make sense. *Pomba* means dove, and *gira* turning – but as we have just seen ngira was a reference to the congregation itself and as such Pomba Gira is a fertile bird spreading its inspiration over the congregation. This was the table of Mary, while the table of St. Barbara was held by the spirit of fire. St. Barbara in Palo Mayombe is syncretised with Nsasi, the *mpungo* (divinely generated spirit) of thunderbolts and lightning. In Candomblé and Lucumi/Santería, St.

Barbara is syncretised with Sángo, the royal thunder in Yorubá cosmology or Oyá his spouse, Queen of lightning and death.

In reality the good Bishop in his account of the tables just says *Mary*, and of those we have many. Perhaps he meant Mary Magdalene but decided to leave this remark ambiguous? If so, it makes even more sense in terms of the holy spirit as a dove, for who was the inspiration for Jesus ben Elohim, but Mary of Magdalene? These are great cosmic patterns of traditional wisdom that are not confined to Christianity, but can be recognised in Christianity. The Holy Spirit manifest is santé – it is the divine intoxication that takes place and the wine of the prophets is shed.

A Path Appears

12 Quimbanda has always been subject to an initiation or a consecration, or as I tend to see it, a coronation. It was not always so. In Bantu/Congo societies the enbanda was simply recognised as such, a person who on the basis of divine dictate was appointed by the people to act as a prophet. In the time of the cabulas and quilombos it was dangerous to reveal your provenance, so initiations and oaths were sustained by the external profane threat. Today, initiations are necessary in order to reinstall the link with a particular spirit retinue and also to safekeep the cult by oath. The oath being given, the secret is cut into the skin of the candidate so he or she becomes an embodiment of these spiritual influences in a continuum. The initiations can range from simple presentations to a fully fledged presentation in the ngira. In most cases the latter is advisable given how off centre the modern world is. This re-linking or *re-ligare* is done by a cunning Tatá's awareness of the needs of the candidate and the demands of the spirit, and is capable of guiding the seeker to the point of the crossroad where he or she makes their own fate. This is never easy, because at this crossroad you are met with fire and obsession, vanity and corruption, reflections in the ever vibrant mirror of existence.

For those who seek to enter into a relationship with Pomba Gira it is important to keep in mind that her voluptuous icon presents a challenge. She is divine wisdom forged in Hellfire. She is the lustful gift given within a shadow of bleeding night that might rain melancholic poison over your life. She is the crossroad between obsession, intoxication, love and death. She is Venus slain and resurrected, and on that day what do you ask of her? Many people approach Pomba Gira due to problems of love. These problems can be of a selfish nature or they can be born of a desire towards unity. Her domain is love and relationships of any kind and she is more prone to manipulate men than women. Women presenting themselves at her door need to prepare for a journey through her mystery that is not always pleasant. I do consider oneiric work to be the better approach for those who are not being instructed by an initiated quimbandeiro. A simple formula for building a connection is by the rite of the dreaming vessel.

13

The Rite of the Dreaming Vessel

On a Friday at noon – in the time of the new moon – you will purchase the vessel. This vessel can be of clay, china, copper or brass. When you purchase the vessel you will avoid any form of bargaining. When you see it you will know it. Prior to this you will at the exact moment of noon, light a red candle for Pomba Gira and offer a glass of red wine. The candle should be anointed with olive oil and while anointing the candle say:

> *Salve Pomba Gira!*
> *Queen of passions*
> *Mistress of all hearts*
> *I anoint this candle in your honor*
> *Guide me well as I journey towards you*
> *Saravá Pomba Gira!*

Upon obtaining the vessel anoint it with olive oil, almond oil and essence of anis, wrap it in red cloth and leave it under your bed or close to it until the Friday closest to the approaching full moon.

On this Friday at midnight, open the vessel and wash it with cachaça or equally strong liquor, like rum, vodka, kleren, moonshine or gin. Place inside the pot three nutmegs, three star anis and three leaves of bay laurel. Place the pot beside your bed level with your head and light two red candles and one white around it. Offer one glass of red wine, one of cachaça and one of coffee sweetened with brown sugar.

You will state from the heart that you seek to know Pomba Gira while you draw with ink on virgin parchment the ponto (spirit signature) of the Pomba Gira you seek to know. This being completed you will pass the ponto over the three flames and allow it to be consumed by the white candle making sure that the ashes are gathered in the dreaming vessel. Let the candles burn while you take a bath and anoint yourself in perfumes. Then go to bed and wait for what the night will bring.

It is also possible to make simple sacrifices at T-crossroads that are in harmony with the kingdom you seek to know. This is done with the prospect of building connection and avoiding entering into pacts and contracts with the spirit. However, even by doing this one is potentially placing oneself in harm's way because a person of low stature and questionable desire will surely still fall prey to her fangs. The best protection in these preliminary approaches is honesty and tranquility. The more wild your soul is, the more this force will be moved to harmonise with your wildness and herein are found wormholes and obsession. She easily calls the attention of the *kiumbas*, the shells and larvæ that seek nutrition from blood, sperm and emotion to maintain their vitality.

A Crossroad Rite

This ritual follows the traditional steps taken to pacify her and seek to commune with her. You will gather on a Monday noon the following items: seven red roses in bloom that hath been plucked of their thorns, seven red candles, seven metres of red ribbon, one bottle of sparkling white wine or champagne and a new champagne glass. At midnight you will go to the T-crossroad elected and you will write the name of the Pomba Gira you seek on the red ribbon. The ribbon must be cut into seven equal pieces in such way that you have written her name seven times per metre. This adds up to forty-nine which is a sacred number as it speaks of completion in the context of Quimbanda and places the work under the eyes of the Maioral (the Chief of Quimbanda) or one of his three generals. You will trace the ponto with manioc flour or present a pre-prepared red cloth with the ponto drawn upon it. Leave your offering of roses and wine on this, and tie the ribbons around each of the seven candles. Place the ribboned candles around the ponto and light them with matches. The remainder of the matches will be given to her at the ponto by pulling out nine matches showing their red heads outside the box and in this manner placed amidst the roses. At this point make your petition by prayer, song and contemplation while filling the virgin cup until the contents of the bottle are emptied. Stay and let her move you, from this point on she is given charge and control – a moment so much more important for a man than a woman, so dedicate this time well. When the rite has been consummated withdraw by taking three steps backwards, turn aboutface and leave with the crossroad at your back. It is important in this sequence that you come to the crossroad for the sake of petition, to give gifts. Not until you understand her harsh nature and the rules of her guidance should you embark on the pactum.

At times requests made to Pomba Gira can appear not to be working: in most cases this experience is due to her working directly on you. This can be either by perceiving you as food, or as someone she graces with her wisdom. She rarely works by placing the request in your lap without any effort. She opens the door to your desire and only when you enter can you claim your prize. It is about give and take, a contract between spirit and your body and soul. The pactum diabolicum is set in motion.

The Western seeker mesmerised by Pomba Gira can engage in these simple steps, keeping in mind that Pomba Gira represents a spiritual legion of great obsessive quality. She is not like the still burning mercurial fire of Exu, she is the sulfur that infests and strangles. For men the experience can do much good, as closeness to Pomba Gira is bound to give a greater understanding of female complexity. If her grace is bestowed upon woman she tends to infuse her elect with too much sensual potency, often leading to wicked, weird and wild situations. The woman she elects will pass through a magnificent spectrum of possibilities that must be mediated by her own stamina and disposition. It is an intense play between desire and comfort; assault and fear are constantly making their moves around the one who drinks from her cup. This means that she can ignite unconditional lust, as suggested by Antonio Alves, and lead to a fall into uncritical debauchery. The chosen woman may be approached by old and lonely men with finances enough to provide a life of comfort, or she may meet the one who completes her and effectuates the *sýmbolon* of union. She always gives choices, as do all spirits who find their dwelling at the crossroad. She throws out keys freely, but ultimately the choices are not hers. In simple terms, the door ajar might seem like an invitation, but it can also be a temptation of unknowable consequences. Choice manifests when two or more roads are laid before you. Your level of wisdom provides the discrimination required and your spiritual growth hands down the intuition needed to make the choice that reaps the greatest rewards.

OMBA GIRA is a celebration of female virtue and power. 19
In her we find a host of mighty rivers revealing how
Woman challenged the world. She is the vixen, the
fornicator, the seducer, the revolutionary, the witch,
the comforter, the lover, the concubine, the confidante,
the queen and the saint. She is Woman throughout time,
mundane and mythical. She represents a particular refrain of
characters and situations that add layer upon layer until we have
a deep understanding of this voluptuous and intriguing woman. It
is crucial that we realise that these refrains reveal her and are not
something we ought to limit her by. Rather, they serve as examples of
how the spirit of Pomba Gira acts upon the world and what forms of
movement it creates. Pomba Gira is essentially a spirit of the erotic,
but she is also a mirror of social agitation projected towards the erotic
as represented by Woman. These spirits often take the shape of *malan-
dros* or rascals, spirits signified by a playful, roguish and tricky nature,
spirits of the streets and taverns. While for a man the malandro is the
proverbial bad boy with an aura of mystery around him, for women
the story is often very different. The woman who takes pleasure in the
erotic and takes pride in being a woman, is easily labeled lewd and

dangerous. There is something threatening about the free woman who refuses to succumb to male dominance and control. Pomba Gira defies any attempt at being controlled by being completely free and shameless in her flowering as saint or sinner. There is no room for guilt in her world as she takes her pleasure with whomever she desires and however she wants. For her the world is a ground of infinite communion.

Her essence is one of extremes. She moves from the ecstasy of the saints through cruelty and abuse to a voluptuous desire for pleasure. The curtain raises on a wide cast of historical and celestial characters as the blood which draws her forms as Pomba Gira. Here we find Mary Magdalene and Venus side by side with Erzébeth Báthory, Joan of Arc and the Iberian exiled witch Maria Padilha. Here is violence, sorcery, mercy and sensual joy.

Until the research of Marlyse Meyer in 1993, the Queen of Quimbanda, Maria Padilha, was considered merely a myth. In researching the protocols of the Inquisition she found her trial and fate documented. In 1713 we find the account of Antonia Maria from the city of Beja in Portugal who was exiled to Angola for two years. After these two years Antonia Maria and what seems to be her tutor, Joana de Andrade, appear in the state of Pernambuco in Brazil. A conflict between the two is mentioned in which Joana leaves for Angola to become more powerful in magic. It is here, in the curse spoken to Antonia we find Maria Padilha mentioned. Joana swears by Barrabás, Satanás, Lucifer and his woman, Maria Padilha and her legions, to engage in a fast until her enemy is destroyed. This curse is of course modeled on the famous Black Fast. Maria Padilha is also mentioned in the romance *Carmen* by Prosper Mérimée which inspired Bizet's famous opera of same name. Her name also appears in the 14th century when she is spoken of as *a beautiful tigress from Hircana* at the court of Dom Pedro I, the Cruel (1334–1369). This would suggest that she was from Macedonia, but given her appearance and voluptuous attitude she was seen as a gypsy. The story flourishes with scandals, with the cup of poison and the disappearance of lovers, with family and officers of the court in a constant battle for the crown. Maria Padilha herself passed away from an illness and there is nothing indicating poison, but who truly knows? What is known is that she was the mother of at least one of Dom Pedro's children. Pomba Gira's rich mixture of seduction, lewdness and sorcery originated from this most infamous personage. She is sorceress and witch, she is seducer and mistress, a dancer in bars, a gypsy and a poisoner – she is Woman – and in particular those aspects of Woman that the world finds challenging and disturbing.

Pomba Gira lives by the Ocean and the Cemetery, she lives at the cabaret, the tavern and on the streets. Depending on the situation she wears different forms like so many dresses. For instance, Maria Navalha (Maria of the Razor) is a prostitute serving the very poorest who are searching for sexual release. In dominating the most dangerous field in this occupation she needs to be fierce, and her razor references the prostitute always on guard and always ready to send abusive clients to their death. You do not seek her counsel unless you have lost all sense of mercy and wish to inflict a swift revenge upon abusers. In contrast to this fierce and uncompromising form, she can take the form of Pomba Gira das Praias (of the Ocean shores) where she is softer and more understanding – still changeable and raging as moon and ocean, but occupied with mending broken hearts and the turmoil of the soul. Pomba Gira can take on qualities defined by tools, such as the razor, as much as natural kingdoms, for instance the ocean and the ocean shore. We recognise her in the female fire acting upon the world in a free unrestrained form.

She is intimately related to Macumba and harmful magic, which ties her in with the reputation of the gypsies as powerful casters of spells. This factor is important in setting out to identify her. She is a spirit of sorcerous talent, both from Europe, Africa and the Roma people. We see the African connection clearly where Joana leaves for Angola to become even stronger in the arts of malefica. The European heritage is quite evident both in her songs and in the writings of famous umbandistas and quimbandeiros from the middle of the previous century where African and European forms of Craft are presented side by side. It is a synthesis based upon similarities that has produced this vibrant and unique cult that shines out in recognition to all four corners of the world. Her predeliction for synthesis gives rise to puzzling forms of Pomba Gira like the Witch of Evora and Pomba Gira Owl, which are not really unique spirits, but rather represent a particular quality of already established Pomba Giras. We also find this in figures such as Marquesa de Santos, Erzébeth Báthory, Lilith, Salomé, Jezebel, Cleopatra, Clytemnestra, Morgana Le Fay, Myrna Loy and even Catherine Tramell (played by Sharon Stone), the protagonist in Verhœven's 1992 production *Basic Instinct*. These are all representations of La Belle Dame sans Merci, as coined by John Keats in his poetic revelry on the Lamia. Here is the seductress and femme fatale who in her wicked ways serves only her own agenda in a hunt for power and satisfaction. But this is only one part of the complexity of Pomba Gira. She is also Eve, Joan of Arc, St. Catharina, St. Lucia and every woman with a vision that goes beyond herself. These manifestations are not necessarily manifestations of Pomba Gira, but rather they express her qualities. By turning our attention to history and myth we should be cautious about claiming direct relationships between, for instance, Lilith and Jezebel, and dubbing these forms as Pomba Gira Lilith and Pomba Gira Jezebel. This would reveal a lack of critical thinking. Pomba Gira is essentially a legion of the dead. It is precisely because of having lived a human life that she is able to understand our condition so well. As struggle and abuse was a constant challenge in the life of the Pomba Giras, she has a particular interest in providing solace for people locked in struggle. She knows better than anyone the nature of our challenges and upon her spiritual resurrection in the fold of Pomba Giras she also gained perspective upon human suffering.

Pomba Gira is the free woman who follows her heart and desire and knows the cost. The various themes from history which we shall look at express particular functions, but we cannot allow the function to identify a new Pomba Gira solely by recognising her presence in historical and mythical events. It is from confusion between function, form and identity that not a little weirdness enters the cult and we get new labels given to the old, and curious new Pomba Giras being born. That these spirits are not overly concerned with the accuracy of labels, but work more through the intent and connection we have made with the particular form, tends to complicate matters still further. Let us return to the example of Maria Navalha, who is a real Pomba Gira of a more recent birth. This Pomba Gira has a story, and her story is related to the function of the razor as a tool of protection against abuse in the realm of danger where she moves. When the historical person who upon death became this Pomba Gira was alive, she was already living in the form of the Pomba Gira Rainha to whom she went upon her death. She took part of her legion and over time gained a unique form as a protector for a particular class of women.

Let us suggest the existence of Pomba Gira Báthory or Pomba Gira Martha Tabram, one of Jack the Ripper's victims, and question if these could be real Pomba Giras. In essence they could, by the evidence of their history. But there is also the question of cult and identity in life. Did these women have access to what we today know as Quimbanda or perhaps a similar cult where a form of veneration could lead to them being adopted into the legion of a particular Pomba Gira Queen? It is difficult to state absolutes in this regard, but what can be said is that as Quimbanda spreads and is made accessible outside Brazil then this also invites a greater dynamic and possibility for expansion of the legions. In such cases, where a spirit is born, tests are carried out to ascertain whether the spirit is truthful, or if it is an attempt to communicate something related to an already existant Pomba Gira.

In Candomblé and Umbanda we find a distinction between the Orixá Esú and the Quimbanda Exu, the latter often called Exu-egun, or Exu of the dead ones. This vinculum is right and true, Quimbanda is to a great extent composed of a herd of eguns or departed ones that return in spiritual form within the cult of Quimbanda. This makes it difficult and erroneous to discard the vision of new spirits as nonsense because after all, ensuring the evolution of the people of the street, cemetery, church and tavern is a vitally important part of the cult. What often gets in the way is the shallowness of mediumistic exploration. By this I mean that at times people display a fascination with some historical figure who then enters them in possession. Now, this can be true in the context of Quimbanda, but I find it pertinent to understand whether the spirit has manifested due to a true calling and vinculum, or whether it is just a psychic fascination with a concept that unfolds in a possession of an equally psychic nature. For example, Martha Tabram can indeed manifest as a Pomba Gira, but she can also manifest by psychic identification. In my experience, I would see a person receiving the spirit of Martha Tabram as receiving Maria Navalha first, and then as time passes and the connection with spirit matures in the proper way, it becomes quite different, that is, a unique spirit taking form in the legion of Maria Navalha under a specific name related to its substance as a human being. Pomba Gira as the wielder of the possibilities of female abundance invites such creative processes. A journey through some of the themes of historical and mythical women can be helpful in deepening our understanding both about who she is, and the dynamic that is at play in the transformation from human to spirit within her legion.

24

Marquesa Domitila de Santos (1797–1867) was the mistress of Dom Pedro II of Brazil. She was the wife of a tailor, but the king was taken with the young girl and they nurtured a passion for many years and gave birth to five children. Her political powers gradually became so great that she served as the gatekeeper to the king and even managed to have an opposing minister exiled to France. Domitila plotted to take the crown several times but in the end she gave up on the king and departed quietly for the comfort of her own mansion in São Paulo. Domitila clearly represents the free woman who makes her own choices, a woman that never falls prey to the charm of men, but seeks to retain her independence. Her impact is seen in Umbanda where her name is mentioned in songs and I have also heard someone commenting on cultivating Pomba Gira Domitila, but void of this historically relevant knowledge. The informant simply saw her as a powerful sorceress, a servant of Maria Padilha. And it is Maria Padilha herself who spans the aristocratic and the rustic. Maria Padilha is the queen without an official crown as much as she is the archetypical European witch. Her fame is due to her efficiency in rituals and the swift execution of desires. The stories about her are many, ranging from her being an aristocratic woman that took her delight amongst men as she wanted to and never entered into marriage but kept her role as a mistress on her own terms. Stories from Andalucía and the witch trials in Elche have been ascribed to her, a most proper reference given the Carthage and Moorish influences in the mysterious city where we find the Lady of Elche, an ambiguous figure veiled in mystery.

Maria Padilha represents the independent woman and she demands respect because she is Woman. She demonstrates, or rather makes the claim, that behind any powerful man we find an even more powerful woman. This should give some indication of the necessary constitution of her practitioners, and also reveal the force field that opens in her embrace. There is an intense web of female complexity woven into the figure of Maria Padilha. We find stories telling of a strong, hardworking woman, beautiful and desired by men, born in the lowest of classes, yet who defied society by virtue of her brilliant mind and seductive charm. The repeating theme is that of the beautiful and intelligent woman who attracts the interest of kings and clergy. Maria Padilha by her womanhood becomes the King's lover and the mother of his illegitimate children. Some accounts tell that she preferred this condition and refused to accept to marry any man, even the King; others say that her crown was denied by politics and jealousy. She is the Queen without a crown spoken of in the reign of King Pedro I of Castilha, surrounded by moors and gypsies, in the second part of the 12th century. In those days the court was found in Seville and it was an auspicious time for the castle as the king was loved and popular. He was charismatic, a brave warrior and a good hunter. Pedro and his men became the subject of the songs of troubadours and local plays. Maria Padilha worked in the court of Seville and with the aid of a Hebrew magician, who made for her a magical mirror of marble containing the powers of Eros, she obtained the King's attention. Dom Pedro was married to Doña Blanca, a woman said to be rather empty of charm and elegance, who resided in France – thus giving ample room for the king to indulge himself with consorts and concubines. When the eyes of Dom Pedro fell on the beautiful and strong Maria Padilha it did not take long before she became the de facto Queen of Castilha, influential as a Queen, but lacking the crown itself. Dom Pedro made no attempt to conceal this romance and Maria Padilha was loved and respected for her charm and elegance and feared for her aptness in the wise arts. The folk stories become infused at this point, Maria Padilha being subject to the interest of the Inquisition which led to Dom Pedro bringing her to Angola where she would learn both the magic of the Bantu speaking people, as well as the magic and mysteries of the Muslims of Angola. This seems however, to be a confusion with a concubine of Dom Pedro of Portugal (Pedro the Cruel) some three centuries later, which led to the exile of Maria Padilha to Brazil. Whether she was first exiled to Africa and then to Brazil, the records are not clear enough for us to tell.

There is also the presence of Maria Padilha as a separate deity in the company of those who accuse Jesus, headed by the high priest Caifás, as well as within a more satanic context. This exiled woman who, according to one account, landed on the coast of Bahia in 1535, ends in legends of a powerful sorceress with the knowledge of the nganga and a Queen of the powers of the night. The gnawa of the moors stirred the blood as she danced and hearts fell into pieces under her charms and potions. It is a story of seduction and fascination, all the power and mystery a self assertive woman could manifest. This happy woman, well versed in dance, divination and sorcery, with a preference for fine jewels, clothes and drink became the prototypical Pomba Gira and her association with the night and dark powers found its reflex in Pomba Gira being the wife of Exu. In many regards Exu is represented by the regal powers that refuse to accept Pomba Gira as the true Queen, and her response is to enslave the King with her seductive powers. So, on this purely material and political level, Exu is born from the domain of the king, namely the social world. The King is he who gives dictates and is the author of events. For now this purely mundane connection serves our purpose well, as we embark upon presenting some famous female portraits from history that will shed light on the nature of Pomba Gira.

Countess Erzébeth Báthory was a Wallachian noblewoman from the 15th century who went down in history as the Blood Countess, an hysterical and vile woman feeding upon the blood of virgin maidens. In the Middle Ages, the Wallachians were derided by the Habsburgs who seized every opportunity to orchestrate situations that would make their besiegement possible. In the presence of this countess again we see Pomba Gira as a strong woman meddling in the affairs of the state, and because of this it has been suggested that Erzébeth was made the scapegoat of mischievous politics. The allegation is disputed, though a grain of truth might be found in it. The well educated Erzébeth with a love for philosophy and language was known to interfere in cases where women were subject to abuse and mistreatment. As such, she could easily have been seen as a troublesome figure capable of restoring a sense of dignity to women in a world where they had none. It might be that the accusations of sadism and torture of a sexual nature enacted on peasant girls in the district were a political tactic. But there is one detail in her story that suggests something quite different. On the 21st August 1612 she was found dead in the castle where she was held under house arrest. Plates of food and drink where everywhere, but untouched. This gives fuel to the fire of her reputed vampire legacy. Could it be that she abducted a number of young maids to serve as food and when discovered it was decided to starve the vampire to death? Erzébeth was a free woman with an apparently healthy acceptance of herself and her sexuality; as an aristocratic widow with great material wealth in a time of tremendous political conflict, she affirms the salient characteristics in the signature of Pomba Gira. Additionally, her husband was rumoured to be a member of the Dragon Order who also suffered injustice, and thus the plot coagulates. It is as if we witness the hand of Pomba Gira moving actors and situations albeit in a distorted manifestation of her nature. Let us keep in mind the sanguine points that connect Erzébeth and Marquesa de Santos as we venture into the realm of demons.

Lilith also represents an archetypical principle that can illuminate the nature of Pomba Gira. She is the Queen of demons in rabbinical lore and has enjoyed fame in the modern discourse of psychoanalysis and feminist theory, representing the dark and forbidden. She was frequently referred to in the plural, as legion, both in Babylonian and rabbinical texts. This evokes the imagery of Lilith copulating with demons and angels by the Red Sea and giving birth to countless demons every night, the *lilot*. She was also known as Tzaphoni, northern one, in reference to the lands of exile, Nod, Cain's field. The biblical account tells us that she was banished because she refused to bow down to Adam and be submissive to him. A rabbinical account tells how God castrated her husband Samael to put an end to their numerous demon spawn. Rebellion and castration are elements through which we can understand Pomba Gira, particularly in her role as Woman of Seven Husbands. She was the first wife of Adam, but in rejecting hierarchy in favour of equality she was banished and surfaces subsequently as Salomé and the Queen of Sheba. The Queen of Sheba, upon visiting the wise King Solomon, brought gifts and grace. Pomba Gira, like the Queen of Sheba, values wisdom and it is upon the wise her gifts are bestowed.

Salomé gained the reputation of being a dangerous and seductive woman in the form of Ishtar. Like Ishtar her beauty, body and erotic power mesmerised Herod to such an extent that he pledged to give her whatever she desired. Salomé asked for the head of John the Baptist and claimed the gift of prophecy via this most potent necromantic gateway. The lure of her dance hypnotised the king, just as legends tell of how serpents cast a spell upon their victim so they succumb to their hunger. In Salomé we find confidence in an acceptance of her powers, and we encounter her again at the crucifixion of Jesus, though now as a woman who mourns the saviour's fate. The general consensus is that the two Salomés are different, and though this might be so in the mundane history, what she represents in this dual role is more important. As Salomé the younger she takes the head of the prophetic gateway, as the older she mourns her role in the greater design. Salomé fulfils a role similar to Judas Iskariot, being appointed the northern station of betrayal, and as such she fulfils the law and makes salvation possible. Here we find the connection between Salomé and Herodias, the strega who holds uncanny similarities with Maria Padilha.

Jezebel who is spoken of in the *Book of Kings* was a Phoenician princess who suffered death by being thrown out of a window or tower. Her corpse was left as food for dogs and vultures. She was the wife of the King of the North (Ahab) and North is, in Talmudic accounts, the perpetual source of evil. This is evident in the further accounts of the Ba'al worship established by the powers of the North, in the city of Tzebub. Here we find another possible origin to the name Baalzebub, the Lord of the North. Since the overthrown Queen and King were subject to defamation, the city was also named in reference to defecation, hence the reputation of Baalzebub being the Lord of Flies. This finds a greater symbolic importance viewing the Lord of the North, her husband joining with her in death in the form of flies feasting on the flesh of the corpse of the Beloved. Yet again we find a strong and self-assertive noblewoman subject to an unhappy fate due to her beauty and womanhood. Seeing the account of Jezebel as a symbol of promiscuity in this light will shed more glory on the grand mystery of Pomba Gira, whilst also parting the veils to a greater understanding of the relationship between Pomba Giras and Exus.

Cleopatra, the Greek Queen who concluded the Ptolemaic dynasty in Egypt, is still a woman reputed for her beauty, lust and seductiveness. Plutarch tells us in his *Life of Antony* that she was not solely a physical beauty but that her real beauty was her charm, wit and sweet voice. In Cleopatra we see an attitude that sets her apart from the previous Ptolemaic pharaohs, namely that she learned Egyptian and adopted Isis as her divine manifestation. It was not common prior to Cleopatra that the ruler of Egypt bothered to learn Egyptian or adopt their deities; instead both Greek and Egyptian were used as official languages of the state so the Greeks could continue to be aloof in the land they controlled. There are also the love children, both by Julius Cæsar and

Mark Antony, who fixed her erotic allure and wrought around her an even more seductive aura. Reading the accounts of Cleopatra we see a wonderful fusion between beauty of mind, heart and body. This combined with her unrestrained sexuality, at least by reputation, is a most proper motif by which to understand the mature forms of Pomba Gira. In Cleopatra, Pomba Gira assumes the role of the independent woman who seduces the world to adore her triple beauty. There is something in the form of Cleopatra that speaks with eloquence of the type of fascination that makes bindings of love and the erotic world possible.

Clytemneſtra, whose name is commonly misread to signify *famed for her many suitors* was a princess of Sparta. She was a daughter of Leda who was seduced by Zeus in the form of a swan to give birth to both Clytemnestra and Helen. There are some variations in her myth, but the one of interest here is the most widely known. In this account we learn that she married the King of Pisa, Tantalus. Agamemnon lusting for both Pisa and its Queen murders Tantalus and the royal infant and takes Clytemnestra as his wife by force, exercising his regal rights. Against this background we find her bloody reputation as she murders Agamemnon with the axe of Labrys. Pomba Gira is often beseeched by women suffering from abuse and like Clytemnestra she can wield perfect revenge upon abusive males.

Morgana Le Fay is yet another woman who evokes images of adultery, seduction and malefica. She is spoken of as an enchantress and a queen in whose veins fairy blood flowed, making her dangerous and not to be trusted. Yet this sorceress, one of nine sisters, is the one accredited with the healing and restoration of King Arthur. We see here a faint whisper of Salomé as Morgana's life opens up into a journey similar to many Pomba Giras of great repute. Morgana at all times supported what was truthful, she served in a way as a mirror for those around her. This combined with a free sexual appetite marked her as dangerous and out of place. In her we find yet another icon of the fatal and lewd woman who threatens the world by defying its insistence on her staying in her social place. Like Pomba Gira she is Woman as she stands in naked glory before you, shamelessly free of guilt, and poisoning the hearts of men with her charm and passion. There might also be a connection here to the North as the sinister kingdom if we consider the tale of Geaint, son of Erbin. In this story we find Morgan Tud being spoken of as Arthur's physician. It has been suggested that Tud might be a Breton borrowing from the Irish *tuath*, which means north and by natural allusion, wicked.

Eve must also be remembered in this presentation of significant women. Eve is both Mother of the human race and Mother of the Land itself, the womb that made death and resurrection possible. Her name is derived from *chavah*, to breathe – in the sense of igniting life in something. It is the wind that raises the soul. As such, the Holy Spirit in the form of a dove expresses the essential nature of Eve as the mother of all life, creating a connection to Pomba Gira as the swirling dove. Curiously, this title of Mother of all Life is one that was given also to Tiamat, the dragon of the cold waters of chaos in Babylonian mythology, as well as to Jahweh's spouse, Asherah. The relationship between the formative waters and the mother of life as it later lends itself to the mystery of temptation and fall is most telling, and contemplation on these matters leads to a greater understanding of the essence of Pomba Gira herself.

Joan of Arc (1412–1431) was a peasant girl from Orléans who from an early age had divine visions. She was instrumental in several important victories during the Hundred Year's War. Her visionary capacity is similar to that of St. Thérèse of Lisieux and St. Teresa of Ávila. With Joan of Arc we see conjoined divine vision and political influence, in the body of a woman. This is an unsettling image in a world of male dominance. She said that St. Catharina and St. Michael were the divine potencies that gave her visions and inspirations. This conflict between divine inspiration and political confidentiality was what set in motion the events leading to her death. In the confused accounts of her trial we meet a woman that insisted on keeping her oath no matter what the consequences. This unwavering character paired with her prophetic nature made this woman a bitter pill for the Church and State to swallow. We find the importance of oath and promise in Quimbanda as well – once word and promise to the spirits is given it should be kept with diligence unless we want to suffer the consequences of the erotic spirit turning bitter and sour. In this we find many dramatic stories of disaster born of a lack of character.

St. Catharina of the Wheel follows in a natural continuum from Joan. She was an esteemed Christian scholar from the 4th century and Joan of Arc ascribed many of her visions to the influence of this saint. Catharina was born in Alexandria to a pagan family, and her father was the governor of the city, so she was of noble birth in a political climate. She converted to Christianity in her late teens and was instrumental in the conversion of many philosophers. The Emperor Maxentius sentenced Catharina to death by the wheel where her spine would break under the torture. Legend tells that it was rather the wheel that broke at her touch, and that she had to be beheaded instead. Upon her death, angels carried her body to Mount Sinai where the Emperor Justinian established her monastery in the middle of the 6th century. Even though the Church has presented the virgin saint as a model for proper female behaviour (chaste and obedient) it is her role as intercessor and prophetess that is of interest here. These are the qualities we find in Quimbanda that link Pomba Gira with saints as much as women of the streets, pleasure and entertainment.

St. Lucia (283–304) is yet another chaste and virginal saint. She had many suitors and all the dowries given to convince her to marry she gave to the poor. One story concerning the loss of her eyes tells that the guards of the governor of Syrachus upon trying to move her and burn her, poked out her eyes with forks. Another story tells of a suitor that admired her eyes so intensely that she simply took them out and gave them to him, asking him to leave so she could focus on a life devoted to God. Her commemoration is on the 13th December and as such she represents the promise of eternal light on the shortest day of the year, but she is also the herald of darkness and blindness. She expresses an attitude found in many Pomba Giras, stern and uncompromising, like the Pomba Giras of the Crossroads.

Lucrezia Borgia (1480–1519) daughter of Pope Alexander VI, the very apotheosis of papal scandals with his debauchery, sodomy and repeated orgies at the Vatican, is the last of the women we shall attend to. In spite of being a shameful chapter in the history of the papacy, it was from the Borgias' example that Machiavelli penned his work *The Prince*. Lucrezia was married to Giovanni Sforza and it was probably this connection that inspired Machiavelli, as the Sforza dynasty of Milan was reputed both for political and cultural excellence, albeit of an uncompromising fashion. It is also worth mentioning that Fransicso Sforza (1401–1466) together with the duke of Milan, Filippo Visconti (1392–1447) commissioned one of the earliest tarot decks. They ordered a set of *trionfi*, what we know today as the trumps or major arcana in the tarot. Lucrezia was subject to allegations of incest, poisoning, murder and lewdness, whilst the truth was that she was well educated and equally secure in her womanhood. We see here three themes coming together as one: the scorned lover, the ruthless one and the merciful one, a complete fusion of the feminine manifested from the flux. It is a story of nobility and sainthood that is subject to cruelty, and about Woman in all her varieties of passion being subject to judgment and resistance at all possible levels. This rich legacy of knowledge and understanding makes the Pomba Giras potentially very helpful allies. The danger lies in the popular adage that *hell hath no fury as a woman scorned.* In this we find the volatile and dangerous shades of her constitution.

Let us comment further on the reference to the north as it occurs in several of the themes selected here. North is invariably given the element of earth or water. This makes sense, as they both relate to the absence of light. Earth closes for the reception of light, while the night waters consume light and give none back. The North as the abode of death therefore fits with both water and earth. Both in the kabbalistic *Bahir* and in the Hebrew scriptures (such as Jeremiah 46: 20) we find references to the north being the place of evil. In medieval trials it was customary to place the accused in the north, the place of accusation. We also find the association of north as sinister in the devil's door found in many churches, a lonely door located in the northern part.

Pomba Gira is the northern one who rises from the earth and water of night with a soul of sulphur. She is the sum of all mortal women who made their mark upon the world. She exalts the wrongdoings against women into a potent strength and by this she challenges the world and all inferior and base attitudes as she exorcises guilt and shame in favour of love, beauty and life.

T HE NAME Pomba Gira has been subject to a wide range 35
of interpretations. We shall analyse the original etymology, but it is also interesting to look at the other variations, even if they are not etymologically correct, as they expose more about her mystery. Most of them say that she is a *whirling pigeon*, which does accord with her function as a twisted dove that turns, in the same way that the Holy Spirit descends. But most likely the name is a linguistic corruption of Mbùmba Nzila, a district of Mayombe in Congo. *Nzila* means crossing, threshold and crossroad, while *mbùmba* literally means mystery or secret, a name which is also given to a class of serpentine spirits that ensure fertility. The connection both linguistically and symbolically with Nkita and Simbi in this regard is too great to overlook. We might say that the nature of Pombonjira in the light of this is *the serpent of fertility that is made fruitful at the crossroad*. But there is more to this, in the legends of the people of Mayombe we also find accounts of a great healing spirit called Mbùmba which is understood as being the act of molding clay. Pottery is used in African cosmology to describe creation and in particular consciousness. Consciousness is often viewed as being made by God's potter. In Kikongo we also have the related word *ndamba* that is

at times used in reference to mbùmba. Ndamba does not have a direct translation; it refers to a state. The state in question is what occurs when two serpents engage in erotic union, a state we can understand as sharing the same vibration as Pomba Gira. We also have the word *mbamba* which means ancient. This ancient serpent, the Mbamba was considered an nkisi of protection for the Loango people and we know this snake as the green mamba, with the black mamba belonging to a forgotten legacy attributed to the spirit we today call Exu.

The mambas are terrestrial diurnal serpents, relatives of the coral snakes, who at night return to their lairs. This pattern is replicated in Quimbanda where Pomba Gira is approached at night when she is in her lair, the spirit vessel made for her as a dwelling. By day a venomous serpent showing herself in toil, trouble and quarrels in partnerships, she takes on a divine form with the arrival of Vespertina, Venus. This should be suggested both by her colour and that the star Venus possessed a significance for the Congolese. In some myths, Mbumba is seen as a pale deity that vomits forth the planets, first the Moon, then Venus and the other planets concluding with the Earth. More often she is a spirit announcing night and dawn and is seen as the star that marks the beginning and end of night, the domain of spirits when humans withdraw. Similar ideas are found in Quetzalcoatl, the feathered serpent who was conceived of as a manifestation of Venus Vespertina and Matutina, hence he was also given rulership over twins. He was given the hieroglyph of the 9th sign of day, attributed to wind in the Aztec calendar. Venus was furthermore given dominion over grace and war in addition to the most important attribute, fertility.

This serpentine imagery is also found undulating in the background of the 16th century Antonian movement in Congo. This movement was instigated by the noblewoman Betlezi (Beatrice) Kimpa Vita, a prophetess who saw St Anthony of Padua as the returning Christ. After finding *nkisi* (relics) of Jesus Christ and suffering a long term illness where she languished between life and death, she was healed and considered herself as resurrected. For her congregation she was the reincarnation of St Anthony, though some said Joan of Arc, but the consensus was to perceive her as Christ reborn as St. Anthony in the body of Beatrice. She made several alterations to the Christian faith, such as adapting the *Salve Regina* to be in honor of St Anthony. She abolished many sacraments, such as marriage, baptism and confession, and engaged in an iconoclasm that cut both ways. Crosses and minkisis were equally subject to being thrown out of their holy places. She saw all this as unnecessary in the new reign of St. Anthony. Each Friday she entered trance and stayed in heaven until Monday where she received teachings she revealed for her followers. The movement took on dangerous proportions as she made use of the kisimbi spirits and the prestigious and influential kitomi priesthood to spread her Mission. Matters became so grave that in 1596 she, her lover and her child were arrested for heresy. The lover and her child were pardoned but Beatrice was twice burned to ensure that her ashes were not used in any attempts to resurrect her inside a spirit cauldron.

Beatrice was no extraordinary occurrence in Congo, in fact the Ngombe and Nkita cults, which possessed the secrets of prophecy and healing, were quite similar in their mediumistic and prophetic aspirations. The difference is that Beatrice had a far larger political agenda. What is worthy to comment on here is Beatrice's connection to the kisimbi spirits. These spirits are subject to a multiplicity of traits which contribute to the mysterious aura this nation has taken on in Haitian Vodou. These spirits are intimately related to the spirit of children, in particular twins and are said to rest at springs and within watery channels and caves as well as underground rivers. They can take on many forms, though both are mostly seen as pythons or as calabashes, which might be a reference to the spirit vessel itself where the *nkisi* (spirit) is given a home and resting place for its resurrection. They function as genii loci and if a place is experiencing unrest and trouble, this is often resolved by appeasing these spirits. They are always present when twins are born and are considered to hold the mystery of animating bones into living sparks of light. It seems to be an animating spirit that works with the sanctity of the earth itself. The animating principle spoken of rests in these spirits as a spirit infested mud, which once appeased and entered into contract with, can be used to animate other things. This in turn connects this mystery

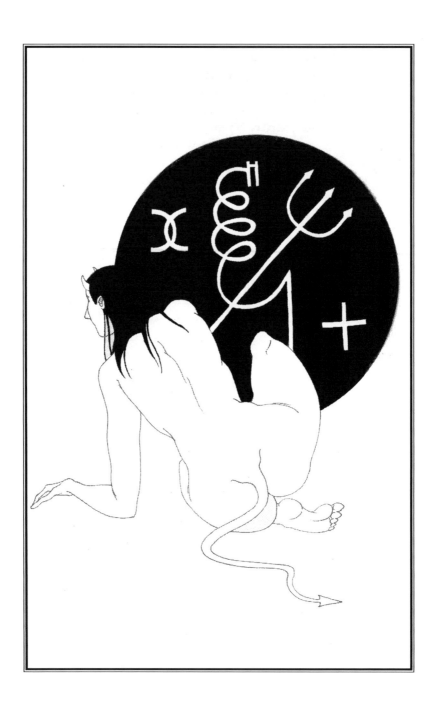

with the owner of the wilderness, the animating principle of all plants and vegetation, fertility itself, as evident from all sorts of rites done with leaves and healing under their powers. It seems that these spirits form the bridge between the worlds and between conditions in the very essence of their being.

We find a connection between these mysteries and Kimpa Vita's St Anthony in Minas Gerais, Brazil in 1749. In this year the Angolan slave Luiza Pinta was tortured and condemned by the Portuguese Inquisition on charges of heresy and malefica. She was accused of being a *calundeira*, which was the pejorative term referring to those upholding their African customs. The term calundueira was used to describe those that went to the kalunga (cemetery) to convene with the dead and therefore practice 'black magic.' There might also be a forgotten reference in this term to someone who held a *caldeira*, a cauldron, the typical spirit vessel used to house nkisi. Like Kimpa Vita, Luiza Pinta was sentenced to the fire and like Kimpa Vita she screamed out for the aid of St Anthony during her fiery torture. We should not forget that possession by saints, like St. Anthony is mentioned in Lourenço Braga's 1956 publication detailing the magical works of Umbanda.

The Star of Night and Day, the Dove of Venus

Venus, goddess of Love possesses many facets. She can be vengeful and sweet, both unpredictable and reliable. She holds the power that makes the world copulate and vibrate. *Picatrix* tells us she is the source of flavour, sound and song and rules the genitals and both menses and sperm. She rules the joining of genitals and the stomach, the seat of appetites and pleasures of the world. She is described repeatedly as smelling good and being fond of dance and clothes and music, and takes delight as much in vice as in healing. Beauty, eating, drinking, all things colourful and pleasant are to her liking. We also know that she is the author of lovers' conflicts, of obsession and of jealousy as well as the most heinous feuds and wars, those that permit everything for the sake of Love. Beauty is the battleground of Venus and she is

Helen of Troy as much as Brigitte Bardot, the object of desire that speaks of decay. The obsession that seeks to possess, and the mother who heals by knowledge of all vices, she is the orgy and she is the ecstatic meeting with God. She is choleric fire and gives birth to ecstasy. Venus is the girdle around Shemyaza/Orion the great hunter, the apples of immortality and the will to live. She is all this and so much more, just as Pomba Gira is so much more than meets the eye. Like Pomba Gira, Venus has her roads or epithets, words that designate specific manifestations of this grand power. It is in the fold of Venus we find the celestial core of Pomba Gira, and three forms of Venus in particular should be highlighted.

First of these is *Venus Acidalia* who used to bathe with the Graces. Her name has been suggested as meaning trouble. This might be evident in the fact that the three Graces are the girdle used by Orion, the great hunter. According to Homer, the Graces were children of Dionysus and Aphrodite/Venus and related to charm, beauty and fertility comingled under Charis, charity. They were Aglæa, splendour, Euphrosyne, mirth and Thalia, joyousness. They were all connected to the mystery of initiation and the mysteries of Eleusis. This connects Charity with Hades.

Then we have *Venus Erycina*, from the city of Eryx and patron of prostitutes. This epithet refers to a Carthaginian city that adopted Astarte as its deity. Eryx, who built this city, was a son of Venus and its origin can be related to the Latin *eschelus,* meaning centaur. The centaurs are perhaps most famous for their abduction of the Lapith women at the wedding of their King. This is an interesting canvas to paint the icon of Pomba Gira upon, as here we find male powers usurping the female. Instead of being used for support and guidance they are simply usurped by the king's appetite for beauty. The dubious etymology of the word centaur is also interesting for our discourse, *ken-tauros* – piercing bull. This can be in reference to the killer of bulls, and signifies a transition from a hybrid between man-bulls, like the Minotaur and the man-horses. The constellation of Centaurus was adopted by the Greeks from Mesopotamia where it was assigned to the fertile Lord Baal. Baal was seen as constantly piercing Mot, the god of Death and drought that later was seen as a form of Pluto. We should add that the astrological sign of Taurus, the bull is ruled by Venus.

Perhaps *Venus Libertina* is the most confusing form of Venus and the most telling, as a smokily lit avenue leading towards Pomba Gira. Libertina is usually translated as free woman. This has been suggested as a case of mistaken identity with Lubentina who lives on in our word libertine. Interestingly, this confused form of Venus can also be related to the *goes* and also funerals in the form of Libitina, the power that releases the soul. Libitina was seen as a winged spirit in a dark hood that took one away on the appointed moment at fate's dictate. She was seen as a bird of prey. This connection with death, Persephone, lust, abduction and seductiveness is once more indicative of the complexity of Pomba Gira. The coin given to Charon, the ferryman, is Libitina. I do not find this paradoxical at all, as the funeral releases the soul into freedom. Love is free and its expression is only restrained by external powers that seek to inhibit it.

41

Pomba Gira as Protector of Land & Temple

It is useful for our present discourse to stay with the Roman myths. I refer here to the retinue of protective spirits, guardians, a term we find frequently applied to the spirits of Quimbanda. The equivalent of a guardian of a specific location, or a kingdom, is genii/genius/daimon. We should also consider that a female daimon or genii was often called a *juno* in reference to the deity Juno, a harsh, strong, sensual and independent woman that constantly challenged her husband Jupiter, but never parted from his side. The genii loci, and often lares, were depicted in youthful and serpentine forms. The naked winged youth flanked by snakes rising from the earth is a typical image of how these spirits were seen. In considering the protective side of junos they were thought of as guardians of womanhood. Take for example the various phases of marriage: we find titles such as Iugalis (protector of marriage), Matronalis (protector of the married woman), Pronuba (protector of the bride) and Virginalis (protector of virginity).

It seems that there was little difference in spiritual substance between these guardians or geniis and lares. The difference was one of degree, evinced by the fact that many lares evolved to a divine status, assimilated with the Roman gods but the geniis retained their daimonic and free nature. As the Roman world evolved, the geniis were more and more considered pagan remnants and were coloured by the demonology of Christianity. Together with lares, geniis and nymphs, we also find another class of spirits, the 'bad lares', larvæs or lemurs that were celebrated in ancient Rome during a three day ceremony culminating on 13th May. The origin of this celebration was, according to Ovid in his *Fasti*, the appeasing of the spirit of Remus who met death at the hands of his brother Romulus. It is said that on the day of Remus' death the patriarch had to go around the household nine times throwing black beans upon the ground to appease the malevolent spirits. The virginal priestesses of Vesta would prepare a cake from the first cut stands of wheat which was given as an offering with the same intent. This is not without importance in our discourse as *ear of wheat* is the fixed star Spica, connected to Venus by the emerald and being partly of Venus' nature. It is my belief that the guardian of geniis and lares were the spirits of Spica. This gives yet another dimension to Venus by the work of the emerald that is rarely commented upon, namely the connection with the malevolent lares, the larvæs. First the cake of wheat is given to appease, then the black beans are thrown around to appease and for oracular purposes. This was followed by clashing bronze pots while reciting prayers and songs to keep the ghosts of ancestors away. It is quite interesting that the term Ovid is using, *ghosts of my ancestry*, is in the sense of shades that cause trouble. It is almost as if he is speaking of the kiumbas in Quimbanda, those malevolent servants of the guardians. We should also point out that dishes made from heavily peppered black beans are frequently given as food for the spirits of Quimbanda. May was considered unlucky for marriage because the spirits of the dead were too numerous, and 13th May was designated by St. Ephrem as the Day of All Saints – the original Roman date for celebrating the dead. Larvæ were a form of angry and hostile lares – both under the protection of Spica who is mediated by the Moon and Venus, the planets that define womanhood. But the rivers of enlightenment do not stop here. We also have the Mother of the Lares, Larenta, who Varro calls Mania. Mania was a Sabine deity, but is also a Greek principle. Plato in his *Symposium* refers to the intoxication of Eros that leads to prophecy as *mania*. It is a state of exaltation that leads to becoming oracular. Naturally, mania was equated with evil spirits by later Roman writers as the world entered the fog of dualist Christianity. Larenta was later reputed to be given children in sacrifice which connects her with the medieval accusations of witches eating children. Ovid suggests that Larenta's origin is found in the nymph Lara, one of the lovers of Zeus. According to the myth she could not keep quiet, so Zeus ordered Mercury to guide her to Hades. On the way Mercury made love to her – some accounts say he raped her, which makes even more sense in the scope of our discourse – and from this union the lares were born. What is apparent here is that the lightning, as Zeus, in conjoining with nymphs, is crucial to the generation of a specific class of chthonic and oracular spirit – due to the involvement of Mercury. In the case of Lara we learn that her tongue was cut out as a punishment for revealing the secrets of the lightning – great symbol of creation and oracles related to destiny – hence the origin of the Manes of silence. We should also note that she gave birth to twins by Mercury, and it is here with the twin Manes, mercurial sulphur in the halls of Hades, we perhaps find a class of spirit that resonates with Pomba Gira and Exu. The Manes were fed blood sacrifices, by placing a black rock in a hole dug in the ground, a practice that exists even today in Quimbanda. The Manes were silent spirits hovering over the stone that barred the underworld from the world of the living; they were in need of mediums and prophets to impart their knowledge and guidance. Hades is a place of silence and the *ad Manes* (dead ones) are silent. The leaders of the ad Manes is Lara, now Larenta, and Tacita, the silent ones, who on account of their mercurial gift enable necromancy to be established by oracles and mania (possession). When Apuleius tells us that *Di Manes* are spirits of the underworld and also of specific locations, he could just as well be describing the spirits of Quimbanda with an almost chirurgical precision. If we note Festus' perception that they are spirits of Inferno or Hell, he is again affirming this conclusion, as does Varro when he speaks of Di Manes as *once human*. In fact, it seems that over the course of the first five hundred years of our common era the distinction between manes and lares was blurred. Even the horrific larvæ and lemurs are united in a broader category as lares which are given a more frightening cast. They are all relegated to Inferno. Let us add that Servius Tullius, sixth emperor of Rome who instigated Larentalia, was said to be fathered by a Lare who was impregnated by a phallus rising up from the earth, the realm of Hades, while she was a virgin. Servius was himself the son of a de facto virgin birth made possible by a merging between the Lares and Hades. It is my belief that amongst these myths we see a memory of the essence of the spirits of Quimbanda. Some are born by Hades' intervention and become spirits, many others are Di Manes and yet others are Lares intertwined with Di Manes.

As society evolved away from the sense of *gentes* (clans) and households upholding the veneration of the Lares, these important local spirits fell away from a centralised cult. They were either absorbed into deities, forgotten or demonised. It is these older agricultural remnants of cults, supported by households and the gentiles, that were banished into obscurity and the twilight of memory. This transition from agricultural cults to state regulated worship generated a divide between the forbidden and the true, between diabolic worship and permitted practice.

This memory can be kindled at the foot of the Dracæna, the dragon blood tree, which is indispensable for generating the spirit vessel of Pomba Gira. Herein lies the memory of the She-dragon metamorphosed into a tree that stretches down to Hades, speaks in the silence of Di Manes and bleeds wisdom and healing. Here, in silence and blood she rests.

The Serpent that animates Death

Pomba Gira can be considered as a principle of fertility, the serpentine principle that animates life in dead things by vision and oracles. We find a direct path in this mystery to kundalini, the snake that awakens us from the slumber of death. This also connects to the practical application of Pomba Gira in Quimbanda, especially in dream work and the development of mediumship. If we look at the concept of kundalini, we find that the serpent within slumbers in the sacrum, or *luz* bone, the proverbial vertebra of resurrection. Kundalini is the serpent of kala time and lunar flow. By becoming conscious, in time, we are also awakening to an original state where we can freely traverse between the worlds in prophetic frenzy and clear perception. This is also found in the icon of Vishnu sleeping in the embrace of the Sesa serpent. His awakening generates the entire universe. This connection with time, primordial becoming and return, as well as prophecy, is a constant theme in serpentine iconography whether of Abraxas, Cernunnos, Vinata, Siva or Hermes Caduceus. We see here a web of healing and stability woven with the erotic, and awakening us to a primordial state where we ourselves become creators in the image of the creative principle. We see this in the ouroborus composed of two dragon snakes, and in the rainbow serpent manifesting in the subterrestrial serpents. The wisdom of creation lives on in the tunnels of the Earth and on the golden islands in Hades' kingdom.

Kundalini represents the potential for an awakening from within the earth. The muladhara chakra or luz bone represents the cross bone of beginning. Awakening here mirrors Vishnu's awakening in a play between micro and macro cosmos. She is the red serpent of the land as she strikes within the body and leads consciousness in a return to its original oracular perception of all worlds. It is here, in the work of the serpent power of the land, we find the importance of gathering dirt and earths from various locations to make the spirit vessels. The unique vibrations of specific locations are brought upon these places because of serpentine ley lines that cross under the earth and generate a unique potency, a kingdom. The snake is the guardian of this king-

45

dom as it also guards knowledge and life, as in the Garden of Eden. But more than this, kundalini is seen as a fire, as is Pomba Gira. She is the fire in your spine that proceeds from beneath the ground. She is the Hellfire from the centre of the earth that crawls upwards along your nerves and transforms your cranial vault into a mausoleum and sepulchre of wisdom.

The Python & Prophecy

In terms of function, Pomba Gira also shares essential attributes with the Drakaina or she-dragon. The Greek *drakein* means to see clearly or sharply, and refers to prophecy and how the medium gazes into realms forbidden to normal sight in order to see more than what is allowed by mundane sight under the Sun. Similar qualities are also given to Python, as is evident from her Delphic temple, the seat of prophecy. Dragons and snakes shared the domain of what is hidden, served as guardians of springs and treasures, and were attracted to the shiny and beautiful. Often seen as intruders upon the mundane order, as something other, both Python, slain by Apollo when he took over her temple, and the she-dragon Echidna, were given domain over corruption and rottenness. Echidna was depicted as a woman with the lower body of a serpent. The consort of Typhœus, together they spawned terrible and strange creatures to torment the earth. Typhœus, dragon of storm and sky mating with the Python underground, a marriage of pleasure between heaven and hell. Typhœus was said to be imprisoned beneath the volcano Etna in Sicily where their union in the world of De Manes breathes fire upon the earth. Typhœus was a giant snake whose head touched the perimeters of the stars, his limbs being all serpentine with eyes of fire and a mouth filled with burning coals. Here is an ancestral memory that the retinue of Quimbanda also partakes of.

When Apollo killed the dragon it is said that the corpse became *python*, rottenness, that is, an oracular corpse. We need to approach this tale as one that expresses the need for restraint rather than banishment. In death, a metaphor for it being given a place of rest and defined space, the dragon reigns forever as the guardian of the roots of the axis mundi. In doing this, Apollo is arresting the flow of time to restore timelessness. In Quimbanda our attention is directed towards the ground when we seek to commune with the spirits or enter possession. Always, it is a rush from beneath that flows up, strikes the neck and pulls us down.

By accomplishing this, Apollo becomes responsible for maintaining life in Pythos, as the Sun is crucial for heating the cold bodies of serpents. This is mirrored in Umbanda with Ogum, often seen as St. George or St Jacques, who is considered the king of Umbanda and Quimbanda. The transition of imagery from Apollo to St George/ Ogum through St. Michael the Archangel, reveals a mystery veiled within one of the many secrets of Quimbanda related to the Maioral. St. Michael is in many ways the Maioral of Quimbanda, although this reveals only a glimpse of the full picture where the slayer and the slain become one. In some houses of Quimbanda that do not lean towards Umbanda, we find St. Michael taking a prestigious and mysterious position within the cult. This would actually suggest Apollo in the form of St Michael and the dragon as being the particular chthonic visionary source that is worked in Quimbanda.

I F WE STARE rapt at the intensely knotted roots that led to Quimbanda being born, we indeed see serpents engaged in love-play and it is here we need to fix our understanding of the cult. It can appear to be a syncretistic tangle and a hybrid as much as it can give the impression of being a system. I believe we should approach the cult as the work of a specific point of power, or a kingdom, that over time has become regulated by a number of guardians and initiates. The social transition of the cult from cabulas to terreiro is demonstrative of the unrestrained soul of Quimbanda as a cult that wrestles itself out of any dogmatic grip. Even if this is the essential temperament of the cult it can also be restrained to a certain degree, as we see in the case of Umbanda. After a decade of working with Quimbanda unrelated to any other cult, religion or framework, I have found that when approached as a cult of mediums and spirit egress it has revealed layer upon layer that shows the cult to be sufficient in and of itself. This means that there is little room for condemning some forms of veneration and exalting others. In this Quimbanda is pragmatic and given to unique expressions, as it adapts itself to the specific constitution of the people that constitute its local cults. I believe this perspective is far more truthful to the soul of the cult than treating it as a religious institution or burdening it with rules and regulations. After all, these are teaching spirits, denizens of the underworld, by virtue of their once human incarnations. Attempts at restraining the cult in relation to 'higher forces' replicates the dyadic arrogance of the Greek and Roman world transmitted into the Christian worldview where heaven is good and the realm of Hades is bad.

It is undeniable that Quimbanda possess a fierce reputation, and with good reason. A form of balance and equilibrium is important to maintain when the cult is worked. After all, many of these spirits are authors of mischief and malefica if treated in such a way that these powers are allowed to manifest. The cult is celebrated with fire, tobacco and alcohol and it is not uncommon to see the practitioner falling prey to the fire and becoming an aggressive drunkard. When this occurs it is a clear sign of the practitioner allowing their own enslavement under the lash of the spirits, serving more as food and a tool for them rather than being in a relationship of tutoring and growth. This equilibrium is perhaps more easy to maintain if one works the cult from a dyadic perspective, where they are seen as bad and dangerous beings in need of elevation. Such an approach also bars much knowledge and even induces a distorted, or at the very least an unbalanced, view of who the spirits are. This much needed equilibrium is maintained by actually being tutored by a Tatá or a Yayá of the cult. Alternatively, one can seek balance in a regular regime of attending wisely to one's consciousness with prayers and *amaci* (herbal baths). I have found that those who work Quimbanda with a foundation in Orisa worship tend to enter with a balanced foundation that serves well when we are dealing with these spirits.

The potential for malefica is not only a reality of the cult, but the power it holds for this is literally breathtaking: the desire for power, to subdue enemies, bind lovers and dominate people. Faced with these temptations it is easy for the immature to fall prey to them. Many go astray and a silent pact is entered into; this is the same complex that gave the *pactum diabolicum* such a bad reputation. In Quimbanda these temptations are presented in order to lure one to look into these

spirits as you would in a mirror. By making us aware of the putrid decay within the human soul and all the powers that would drag us down to Hell, these spirits entice us to make a wise choice. This decision hinges on accepting them as tutors rather than servants or slaves. Doing so will initiate a journey on which you will be confronted by yourself in alternately wondrous and depraved ways. Enigmatic and troublesome situations will arise, first as challenges to test your constitution, then as lessons that open into a greater understanding of life and its mysteries.

All the Queen's Kings

The relationship between Exu Rei and Pomba Gira is a complex one. Here we have the myth of Maria Padilha who was seen as manifesting successively through the early and late Middle Ages, consummating seven marriages in all. Each of these husbands was taken to her kingdom as her attendant. None of them was her equal and thus she gained the reputation of being the woman of seven husbands. The only lover that could withstand her force was Exu. Again we can recall Hellenic myths, noting a similarity between the relationship of Pomba Gira and Exu and that of Hera and Zeus. Only Hera/Juno the wife of Zeus/Jupiter could take Zeus in all his glory, yet turned instead to Hades. Here we meet once more Typhœus and Echidna, who were able to come together and consume each other as a subterranean mirroring of the celestial realm. Only Exu Rei himself, the King Snake, can unite with Pomba Gira, the She snake, and in this act each is empowered by the other. This mirror effect might be more understandable if we turn to Vedic tales of the *asuras*. The asuras were the children of Diti, or Earth, and the sage Kasyapa, meaning vision. In Vedic times, the asuras were seen as the guardians of the world of matter, morals and all social phenomena; this makes Varuna the chief of the asuras, the author of the law. As the world decayed into the Kali Yuga, an age of dissolution and confusion, the vileness of the asuras was upheld by that of the morally blind societies they were set to guard. The asuras are also said to be the daughters of Daksha, often depicted in serpentine forms. They are also intimately linked to a class of redeemed asuras, the *yakshas*, ruled by Kubera, who are considered guardians of all that is mysterious and marvelous, as well as the earth's treasures. They are often connected to *rāksasa*, a night-wandering class of spirits, and the *nāgas*, or serpents.

What we find as a continuing motif is that the secret and mysterious world of asuras, yakshas, nagas and night spirits also have kingdoms and rulers. They mirror the revelations of light from heaven by contracting this light into mystery. It is indeed as René Guénon said: *as above, so below – but opposite*; and herein lies the mystery of King Exu and his Queen, Pomba Gira. If we envision them from this perspective, we can see how the mother is subject to constant veneration. As the royal womb she is the one that is guarded by seven kings. The connection between serpents and the guardianship of the mysterious forces that move morality both in society and the underworld ties in beautifully with King Exu and Queen Pomba Gira. Because of this they know all our human weaknesses and requirements, and are thus perfect reflections of our constitution and station. It is on account of this that we meet no judgment from Pomba Gira. She understands what we are going through. We confess to her not because we want absolution, but in order to understand, and this understanding we are searching for she gives willingly – though erratically. You may be the wisest of saints or the most depraved of sinners, she does not judge, for she is the mirror of all the possibilities humanity holds. She only demands your honesty.

Pomba Gira is solace, she gives comfort in times of distress and she is the one that ignites joy and hope when life is trouble and hopelessness. As such she is drawing upon the icon of the archetypical witch, for good and ill. Over the years I have come to see her in this light, as the spirit of solace. The comfort she gives may not always be pleasant, but it is always what one needs. She is manifested in the plant genus solanum, and it is here we should turn our attention when we want to approach her outside of cult and rite and in a direct and intimate manner. Not only the solanum but also the ipomea and convolvulus are loved by her and it is by going to the kingdom of solace we can find ways not only of inviting her into our lives, but inviting her in the knowledge of what she can do.

She is a stern mother that gives her children what they need and what they desire, though in crooked ways. She is passion as a teacher, and thus first we are drawn towards her erotic and seductive imagery. I will give here a personal account of my life with Pomba Gira using plants as guides. This is the way I find most suitable to speak about her soul as it flashes forth in the cult of Quimbanda.

Herbas Diabolus Solatium

When we venture into the domain of the nightshades we enter into the domain of Fate and serpents, the kingdom of the Devil himself. The nightshades are powerful remedies, equally powerful killers and they can be guides to the other kingdoms. Asclepius the healer bears twined about his staff serpents of the earth that resonate with the serpents Zeus throws to earth in the form of lightning. It is the nightshade we see in the eyes of modern day cinematic demons. The nightshades are the garden of otherness that reflect our soul, our human condition and the forgotten aspirations that have always been a part of our humanity. The poison of the nightshade is the poison we accumulate through a life lived in falsity and denial. On the journey through the garden of night we first meet the lovely Belladonna. Plant genii of Dama da Noite and the whole kingdom of the Lyre, and she tells us:

> *I am Beauty*
> *And I am the burden of all sins*
> *I am the garden at night*
> *At my groin it all begins*
> *The beginning of true sight*
> *I am the apple and the blade*
> *The caress that disappeared*

I am the memory of life as it shall fade
All the beauty that you feared
You are in my garden now
Betwixt worlds you are
In this instant your soul shall grow
I am Beauty
Resting at your brow
Shall you receive me Now?

She is the bittersweet nightshade (*solanum dulcamara*) spoken of in
Sappho's poetry. She is the shade that covers the plants of day, creeping as a serpent of comfort over the solar plants. She is Atropos whom
the Romans called Morta. She is the atropine in the Belladonna that
makes the eyes black with beauty. Here we find Fate whose mother is
said to be Themis, the guardian of morality and law amongst humans, the divine dictate in its harmonious parts, as in the relationship
between Varuna and the asuras. The father of the Fates or Moiræ
was Zeus, he who wielded serpents from heaven, and the Fates were
Clotho, whom the Romans called Nona or the Ninth, which resonates
with the ninth house of heaven ascribed to study and learning. She
was the one that came in the 9th month of gestation, she who gave the
appointed share of life and luck to the newborn. We have then Lachesis, called Decima amongst the Romans referring to the 10th house of
heaven that brings fame or disgrace. Her name means the one that
gives chance and it is here we find luck. She is the crossroad of chance
and is our constant companion in life. In the end we meet Atropos,
the inevitable, Saint Death herself. Your allotted share always gives
chance, and death can be black, red or white.

Some sources say that Zeus fathered the fates with Ananke, necessity, or with Nyx, the Night of Movement. But in reality we see here
a triple motherhood. Themis is the mother of Clotho where the law
unique to us is meted out and Ananke is the mother of Lachesis as we
need power and fire to take chances. Nyx is the mother of Atropos,
because herein lies the veil that separates the living from the dead, and
the world beneath the sun from the world beneath the moon. Zeus in

his more primal or rustic form is the celestial serpent that animates life on earth. He marks the beginning and the end and the serpent's vertebræ is the field of chance.

As we see, Pomba Gira is chance as it spreads out in the houses of night and becoming. She is the Woman of Night who entertains guides and sends you to your final rest. She is the Queen who tends the devil's garden and as she is Queen we are solely occurrences in the garden of chance.

In the garden of the nightshades we meet the purple devil also known as Malevolence (*solanum atropurpureum*), a plant with the most seductive fruits and equally appalling thorns. Cattle are known to have fallen prey to its fruits and crossed over to the land of earth, hence its epithet of *the five minute plant,* referring to the speed of its murderous action. It is however a most useful plant in works with Maria Navalha and Rosa Caveira when done in conjunction with Exu Omulu or Exu Caveira. A name, or even better a volt (a charged item such as hair, nail, fluids, cloth, skin &c.), from the intended victim, with the right intent placed inside its fruits as part of an offering is bound to bring problems to the target.

A close relative of the Malevolence is the Apple of Sodom (*solanum mammosum*) which can be used for a variety of ends, from getting pregnant to inspiring lust. Small amounts prepared at the foot of Pomba Gira and slipped into food and drink will make men docile and willing, whilst in women it will stimulate ovulation, alongside the docile lust the plant induces. This gift given in abundance will certainly make the docile permanently lustful in the halls of Hell.

Yet another fruit of the night that demands care is the Melão St. Cætano or Devil's thorn (*solanum pyracanthon*). This is a most wonderful remedy for those who find themselves wronged, as it will ignite in the victim such an unbearable heat that he or she will fall passive under its influence.

A relative of this mischievous plant is the Wolf Apple (*solanum lycocarpum*). These fruits are edible and serve as a source of food for the Brazilian wolf. In fact they are in a symbiosis of mutual need.

In the fruits of the mature plant they share a soul, but outside this the plant invites a shift in temperament where the bestial part of the human constitution takes over, and is thus related to the mystery of lycanthropy. The fruit is rich in tannins, a compound that gives good wine its savour of nobility. Taken young it will not impart this nobility but will lead the consumer into a revelry of passions devoid of virtue. It is in this unripe state the transformation between wolf and man occurs. This reveals a plant that when unripe can be used to sow havoc between couples, as it stimulates the surfacing of primal states that often distort the truth. That being said, the ripe fruit is a powerful vermifuge and can be turned into a marmalade as part of a healthy diet. But this kingdom that also includes potato, eggplant and tomato does not stop here. We need to journey further into the kingdoms of death, healing and chance.

Peppers (capsicum genus) are yet another solanum in the nightshade family subject to ambiguous uses. The Incas considered peppers to be highly disruptive and refrained from ritual use of the plant as they felt it would repel spirits. This use of peppers as a repellent is similar to the use of garlic, and both in the Caribbean, Latin America and amongst Louisiana hoodoo practitioners we find the belief that bundles of red peppers possess wonderful repelling properties, whether of the evil eye or baneful spiritual influences. Its powers as a repellent are well documented in folk medicine where it is used as a vermifuge, stimulant and analgesic. Alligator pepper is chewed in West Africa prior to enchantments and prayers as the power of fire will bring the words to manifestation faster. The red chili is taboo for the Orixa Esu, and it is said to provoke an untameable and hostile fire, whilst Orixa Ogum, the Lord of iron and strength is happy to take them. Red pepper also keeps plagues, such as ants and invasive hungry bugs, away from plants. In Quimbanda red peppers are used as a fumigation to banish kiumbas and hostile spirits and is a priceless ingredient in the standard offering, the padé. Through the pepper we discover the alliance Pomba Gira and Exu have with Ogum, and by the simple play between taboo and acceptance the Orixa Esu is eliminated from the design of Quimbanda. When giving peppers it is actually the strength of the blacksmith, the lord of iron that is invited to support our gift. A bush of red peppers planted outside one's door and regularly presented with prayers for protection will grow into a fierce protectoress of the house and it's dwellers. Peppers are apparently closely tied to death. In Vodou we find peppers appreciated not only by the Petro nations, but also by Baron Samedi – the Lord of the realm of Death. There is a sacred union that takes place between red peppers and night, where the pepper is like a beacon of flame that attracts these spirits, infusing them with vigour. This is also the effect they have in Quimbanda. Nine red peppers containing the name of someone you seek to draw closer, covered with honey, cloves, and roses, is a proper gift for Pomba Gira that will quicken the fire in the target and makes his or her fire sweet and hot. This fire will be directed towards you if you apply strategy and stay close to the target in the weeks after doing this working.

Another indispensible nightshade is *Tobacco* (*nicotiana*). This plant was introduced into Europe in the 15th century. It was said to cure a number of illnesses and it is, in fact, a good medicine depending upon the age of the user and the purity of the leaves. In moderation tobacco actually possesses properties that strengthen the immune defence and combat cancer, but as with all nightshades, excess will make it a killer. It is salubrious for the male in particular, though women more easily succumb to its allure. Tobacco has been used for recreation and medicine as well as in ritual for several millenia. In Brazil it is used amongst *pajés*, the native cults and forms of worship, as a sacrament, as a means to invite spirits and for divination. In Quimbanda it serves as a sacrament and it is also said to earth the spirit when it is coming down and make it settle well in the medium. Pomba Gira tends to favour perfumed but strong tobacco, cigarillos of good quality flavoured with mint, vanilla or cherry. Cigarettes and cigarillos are a constant presence in her offerings. The saliva or blood of someone that is sought after and smoked by Pomba Gira, with the intent of fascination, will surely bring a stirring in the object of desire.

Henbane (hyoscyamus niger) is also a plant of solace, and with its beautiful flowers arouses the interest of Pomba Gira. Throughout history it has been used as a medium for divination and possession. Ales (pilsner) were brewed from this most intriguing shade of night giving the ale a slightly bitter taste but also unleashing inspiration and a sense of connection. Legends tell that it is best harvested by a naked maiden who is under possession of the spirit, making the plant exceptionally favourable towards women in its naked glory. During the Middle Ages we find reports by the Inquisition in which this plant is presented as a means for stupefying victims. So widespread was the use of henbane that the Inquisitors in Germany and France would convict people for malefica on the mere presence of this plant in their gardens.

At the root of the nightshades we find *Womandrake (mandragora officinarum* of the purple strain) which to the Arabic world was known as *djinn eggs*. As the name still attests, this plant is sacred to dragons and serpents. It is an oracular root ascribed to Circe. It has also received other charming names, like Satan's Apple and also Love Apple, due to its aphrodisiac qualities. The root was sought after in the Middle Ages both for its medicinal qualities and for poppet magic. The fruits are also known as Aphrodite's Apples, a fruit she shares with her sister Hecate and partakes of under the name of Venus Urania – the Love Queen of the garden. As such we find in the Womandrake a plant that encompasses the totality of powers found in Pomba Gira. But in her garden we find yet other green mysteries that will shed light upon her greatness.

Aconite (aconitum napellus), also known as Wolf's bane, is reputed to be of Hecate's own creation and was used by Medea in an attempt to murder her husband's son. It is said to be an ingredient of the witches' ointment, but its most significant use is rarely discussed, namely as an animator of what is dead. Its deadly qualities know no effective antidote and as it gives death to what is living it gives the life of wolves to what is already dead. It is an herb that can be used in solidifying the presence of all Pomba Giras of the cemetery.

Fig (*ficus carica* and allied species) evokes the presence of wolves, as it gave shade to the she-wolf that suckled Romulus and Remus. The people of Cyrene held Saturn to be the author of the tree and thus crowns of figs were made for the officiating priesthood when sacrifice was made to him. Together with the grape it was sacred to Bacchus, a deity of libertine repute, but in this regard must be seen as hearkening back to an original state of freedom. In the Garden of Eden fig leaves were what denoted man as fallen. The fruits can be used as offerings to all Pomba Giras but is particularly sacred in the mystery of the Queen of the Fig Tree.

Dog's Mercury (*mercurialis perennis*) also makes up part of the garden, not only by its association with the divine psychopomp but because of the blue dye produced from the plant or its relatives, such as the African Waji taken from the tree Indigofera (*leguminosae papilionoideae*). It is integral in Quimbanda and crucial when vessels are made and initiations carried out.

Poppy (*papaver somniferum*) also known as Opium poppy is used as an incense, and as offerings in the name of people one seeks to influence when Morpheus spreads his veil over dreamers. It was a plant sacred to Ceres, fair lady of the harvest, mothers and fertility and also mother of Proserpina which invites the necromantic and fertile qualities of this plant of the mothers of the land.

Rue/Arruda (*ruta graveolens*) takes its name from *reuo*, which means *to release, to banish*, due to its amazing powers of expelling illness, both of the spirit and the body. In Brazil it is a plant much favoured by the benzedeiras and it makes part of the patronage amongst Italy's stregones and stregas. The plant is at times attributed to St. Lucia and is said to be a universal antidote if taken in small portions over a period of time, giving immunity from all forms of hexing and evil eye. In antiquity it was one of several plants that were called *moly*, a most potent antidote against the evil eye. It is a plant suitable for fumigations of

the home and temple. A branch from the plant carried behind the ear or in the shirt pocket is a powerful ward against hexing and envy.

Roses (*rosaceæ*) are a large family and the most praised offering to Pomba Gira, who prefers them thornless and in red or white silk ribbons. Legend gives this plant an important relation to Venus as it was the blood of her beloved Adonis after being gored by a wild boar that was turned into this flower. The rose was also attributed to Bacchus, as well as Flora and Chloris, joyous nymphs who announced the spirit of spring, fertility and merriment. The rose is love, but also love's sadness and the darkness of passion. It has been taken by Pomba Gira in the guise of both Queen of Love and mistress of the lovelorn ones as her most prestigious gift and medium for her many workings. We should also mention that many representations of Flora in art evoke younger forms of Pomba Gira. No gift to Pomba Gira is complete without the presence of roses.

Blackberry/Amora (*rubus fruticosus*) is given occasionally as gifts for Pomba Gira, both fruits and leaves. Legend tells us that when the Devil was thrown out from heaven by Michael he landed in a blackberry bush. Furious with the outcome of the celestial battle he urinated on the fruits, hence the British legend that blackberries should not be picked after Michaelmas (11th October). This gives the sweet and dark fruit a most interesting connotation in Quimbanda and can be given to both Exu as well as Pomba Gira to arouse their fire.

Cinnamon (*cinnamonum*), like the rose, is bound to the domains of love, but loves of a more serene type. In the biblical books ascribed to King Solomon we find cinnamon alongside cassia and myrrh in an ointment for body and the bed where the lovers' embrace takes place. The same herbs were also common gifts to Apollo. Moses was similarly instructed to make a holy oil from these plants. In Rome its use went beyond the lovers' bed and worship, and was also used in funerals – usually of the rich, since it was so costly. Names inscribed on cinnamon sticks and given to Pomba Gira on a bed of honey or peppers with 21 red roses can send Eros to a couple as much as Proserpina, so choose carefully the gifts you give.

Cloves (*syzygium aromaticum*) are warm and aromatic nails of healing and love. They can be used together with several fruits and the nails should then be placed with great intent and presented within a padé for Pomba Gira. This will sweeten her, and your request will be literally nailed at her feet. Due to its stimulating and analgesic properties it is also a plant that gives solace from many infirmities such as overflow of mucus and impotence. It is also possible to make a drink for Pomba Gira by infusing cinnamon sticks and cloves in dry red wine and allow it to steep for a week. This is a most precious gift for her and calls upon her desire to give comfort and sweetness. In Nigeria cloves are ascribed to the Orixa Ogum and infusions of cloves are used as a remedy to correct imbalances of the stomach.

Orange (*citrus* genus) is occasionally used in the cult as well, the fruit can be offered, though more sought after are the flowers and leaves that can be turned into an invigorating amaci that fortifies the reception of spirits for the medium. It is equally well used as a purgative after hard workings, in this instance with the addition of rue.

Apples (*malus* genus) and *Pomegranates* (*punica granatum*) have very interesting affinities with love, seduction and the underworld. The pomegranate was the fruit that seduced Persephone to wed Hades, by her eating the seeds of his pomegranate – a sexual allusion. In works of seduction and binding both pomegranate and apples can be used in various ways. The apple for instance can be parted in two and the names or volts of the people one seeks to bring together are placed in the hollows left after removing the seed capsule. The seeds of the pomegranate can be harvested carefully and placed on the fire slowly with the intent of making a man lustful. The roasted seeds are then returned to the fruit which has been anointed with the blood and saliva from the one who seeks the fire of the aroused man. This is then given to Pomba Gira on a bed of roses. The apple has also been associ-

ated with the fruit of the forbidden tree of the knowledge of good
and evil that led to the Fall from the Garden of Eden, and can be used
equally well to bring a couple together as for works of separation.

Guiné (*petiveria alliacea*) is considered something of a wonder plant
in Brazil. It is said to cure everything from rabies and poisoning to
syphilis and paralysis. It is a plant which is a constant presence in
Quimbanda due to its magnificent properties, both in an infusion and
as an amaci. The garlic-like root serves as a potent repeller of negativity when turned into a *patua* (talisman) or hung over one's front door.
It is frequently used to wash implements of the cult and presented as
part of many *despachos* (workings).

Bamboo (*guadua angustiflora*) should also be mentioned as the tree
of ancestry and death. It is not so commonly used nowadays as it was
in the past when the stems were commonly shaped to hold malefic
sorcery. The fresh buds can be used to make a healing infusion under
the ægis of Pomba Gira de Angola.

Prunus counts a whole array fruits reputed for love and lust, like
cherries, peaches, plums, apricots, nuts and almonds. They are used
to heat what is cold and are proper gifts to give Pomba Gira when we
seek to reunite with lost lovers or bring couples together. They can
also be used as offerings when we seek advancement in society, whether amongst family, groups or at work. A padé rich in honey, nuts and
fruits given at the crossroad of Pomba Gira on Monday nights under
the waxing of the moon is sure to bring your desires to fruition.

Laurel (*laurus nobilis*) is used in Quimbanda for works of battle, combat and victory. One's own name written on the leaves and
presented in a heavily peppered padé along with black beans, and
the name of one's enemy inside a piece of raw beef, can be used to
subdue enemies. This working belongs to the people of the crossroad
and streets. The myth ascribed to the laurel should be well known,
as here we find Apollo challenging Cupid himself. In a demonstra-

tion of power, Cupid shoots the nymph Daphne who is following the divine discourse in hiding and collapses at the feet of Apollo who falls madly in love and tries to ravish her. Daphne's father, the river deity Peneus, transforms her into the bay laurel to avoid her falling victim to Apollo's obsession. Given this myth, the laurel is also suitable in the conquest of hearts.

Basil (*ocimum basilicum*) can be used to spice padé given to Pomba Gira. Its connection to the basilisk or dragon is most interesting due to its common use of bestowing tranquility of heart and mind – to paralyse, as the basilisk stuns, the circle of useless thoughts and fears. It is not only a dragon herb, but also a herb for love to such an extent that the plant can be favourably used in the preparation of the spirit vessels. An infusion of basil with coconut water gives solace to whoever is in distress.

Anis (*illicium anisatum*) and *Fennel* (*fœniculum vulgare*) are indispensable in the cult of Pomba Gira. It is said that Prometheus brought fire to man with the aid of anis which gives the plant a crucial importance in Quimbanda. Fennel holds the power of repelling evil spirits and is the sacred herb amongst members of the horsemen's word society. It is apt at controlling anything wild, be it beast or spirit. This use is also seen in Quimbanda where anis is said to calm down the spirits and make them agreeable. In Europe, fennel was used to guard keyholes, to ward off bad spirits, and hung over the front and back doors of the house. Fennel can also be used in workings where one seeks to control an opposer.

Mints (*mentha* genus) all have in common that they were beloved of Pluto/Hades and consequently Persephone turned the nymph Mentha into the plant we know today. The plant is commonly used as an infusion to rub sacred tools and spirit vessels with, which is said to stimulate the spirits of death. This is in harmony with its medicinal qualities. It is clearly a plant of Pomba Gira due to its ability of fortify the production of estrogen and can render men impotent and effeminate. We should also recall the abortive qualities of *mentha pulegium*, better known as pennyroyal.

Nettle (*Urtiga* genus) is seen by many as the true manifestation of Pomba Gira. It is always one of the herbs used to invite the spirit to be seated in its vessel. I have never seen any exception to this, and deem it as a rule. It is said to bring strength and power along with serenity and presence for Pomba Gira, and this quality makes it, along with anis, most crucial to receive the spirit with. It is worth mentioning that nettles when they sting first release histamine and then serotonin. It is a pleasure-in-the-pain plant, as shown by the Roman use of flagellation with nettle to cure rheumatism and asthma. Anansi, the Asanti spider deity, is connected to the nettle which he uses in works for the seduction of a princess. The saint Milarepa is said to have eaten only nettles during his meditations and as he is an icon of the acceptance of life's harshness, we find yet another divine quality within nettle that deepens our understanding of its importance in Quimbanda.

Corredeira (*borreria* genus) is a category of plants that are said to possess the unique quality of consuming light. It is a succulent, a creeping relative of the cactus. There are at least a handful of plants in Brazil that are referred to as corredeira, all with intoxicating and poisonous, although rarely deadly, qualities. It seems that the Queen of this species is the plant called Crown of Christ (*euphorbia milii*) in Brazil. This plant is said to be the crown of thorns given to Jesus Christ and thus enables the legions of Quimbanda to usurp divine powers. As such it is a plant most favourable to use when one seeks to overthrow someone or steal something. It can also fortify possession, especially by those spirits who live at the great hour and is especially sought after by the Queen of the Seven Crossroads.

Abre Caminho (*bacharis* genus) is a species whose name has been given to many plants that share a feather-like or broom-like appearance. This has led to species not classified as baccharis being used as Abre Caminho. The name of the plant, *to open the way*, is perhaps more important to focus on; we should see it as a name designating a function in the flora. This means that any creeping plant with feathers or brooms or the shine of centipedes are favoured as an *abre caminho*. These plants often have small white or pink flowers. We also have several weeds that prove to be amazingly resistant as they break through stone and concrete. These plants by their rustic and forceful nature open a way, and in my opinion should be valued for this purpose. Their use in ritual is to open whatever is blocked and are particularly attractive to Exu Tranca Ruas, but appreciated by all Pomba Giras as they resonate with her metaphysical complexity.

The name *baccharis* is a reference to Bacchus, and here we find an intriguing route into his mystery as the one who never truly dies. He seems to be devoid of life, only to resurrect. Such associations make this plant a constant companion in the cult as the road opener. If one seeks to open oneself to spirit or open up opportunities the plants that carry this quality will serve us well.

There is one last plant that should be mentioned, even if it does not make part of the traditional garden of Quimbanda. This is the *Devil's Tobacco* (*lobelia tupa/inflata*). This plant from North America was used to treat asthma and respiratory disorders. It has also proved beneficial in the treatment of cancer as well as drug dependency, especially on chemicals. Lobelia is a nerve depressant, which might explain this function. I would count this plant in the fold of plants of solace and it is not without reason that this tobacco was used for the pipe of peace. I have found this plant to be excellent when we seek to calm down situations and people. It also possesses the property of purging environments of hostility and is an herb that can be used favourably in any works concerning the line of Souls.

·

And with this our walk through the garden of Pomba Gira is at an end. As we can see from this account there is a certain vibration shared amongst her plants: they all give solace, love or passion. This presentation should not be seen as the absolute herbal, but an introduction from which to venture on. She is never more limited than the limitations we give to her, which is the message of convolvulus and ipomena, way openers, for Pomba Gira's vanity and potency.

A Retinue of Passion and Blood

T HE RETINUE of Pomba Gira is one of passion and rushing blood. Her minions are myriad variations on the theme of passion as it resonates with places of power and potential dwellings for the spirits of Pomba Gira. She is passion in all its forms, and she is the fascination in seduction and attraction. ¶ Any irrational emotional outbreak can speak to us about the presence of a 'pagan' Pomba Gira which harmonises with her faint origin amongst the kisimbi as a spirit that often brings turbulence if not handled with care, understanding and precision. She is represented by the crossroad, the T-crossroad in particular, which is the traditional symbol not only of spirit merging with matter but also the place where chance and decisions occur. When we start to contemplate the idea of the crossroad, not solely in its mundane manifestation but as the symbol for choice and chance, we see a great number of possibilities for manifestation taking shape. The retinue of Pomba Gira is fixed in relation to the Nine Kingdoms and the established queens. Beyond this, the dynamic interaction between death and passion adds disincarnated spirits to the retinue. These are usually traits of existing Pomba Giras which develop in the court of a specific queen. They can also be kiumbas, spirits lacking in light and direction, similar to larvæ. The Pomba Giras are perhaps more similar to the lares of Rome than anything else – a spirit herd not much different from the kisimbi. This means that technically new Pomba Giras can take shape in time but the tendency is that the queens provide some sort of regulation of the unfolding of new spirits gravitating towards particular qualities.

These spirits have a resonance with another African mystery, namely what the Yorubá calls *ajé*. Given the complexity of this mystery we find many errors and misconceptions creeping in. Ajé are envisioned as birds that are moved by the heat of the belly. The belly is seen as a cauldron whose appetites drive us towards having our hunger, real or imagined, satisfied. Ajé is also a word that is used in reference to the power of witchcraft and is said to dwell in the branches of certain trees. In the Yorubá faith, known as Ifá, we find this concept tied in with a spirit called Iya Mi Osoronga. Her name contains a mystery that is commonly described as *Our Mother who is the Lady of the Birds of Night*. This mystery is integral to understanding Ifá, however in this context it will suffice to present the attributes of this Queen of passion. Her birds are released in the colours of black, red and white – the dominant colours of Quimbanda. We find similar resonances in the cult of St Muerte, an affirmation of the presence of tradition as revealed within the mystery of Woman. In Quimbanda, white is ascribed to all works regarding the line of souls and is concerned with healing and positive spirit contact. Speaking of the ajés, the color white is that of mercy and creativity. The colour red is given to Pomba Gira and works of seduction and attraction. Amongst the ajé, the red ones are those that feed upon fear, anger and passion while the black ones are those that bring terror, death and misfortune. In Quimbanda, black is given to Exu as the protective veil of night for her fire. Black is also associated with the waters of night and the coldness of death.

If we approach Pomba Gira using the conceptions we find amongst the ajé we can see her as gatherings of birds that take their power from the serpent beneath the roots of the tree they have chosen as their dwelling. This also reveals another possibility for spiritual reproduction. The fertile dove reveals Pomba Gira's ability to regenerate and recreate herself in conformity both with natural kingdoms and from human passion and hunger. Just like the snakes coiling at the root of trees form food for the ajé – so too do our passions and emotions. Ultimately we are the authors of peace or discord while the ajé execute their role in the great design. The condition of our soul decides what we attract to us. In Yorubá mythology the mother of ajé is seen as a motherly darkness that speaks through the birds. Hence, all trees where birds find shelter, and especially those with twisted branches, belong to her. The ajé share several qualities with the kisimbi, but while the kisimbi is of water and earth, ajé is of air and night as it manifests in nightmares and fear.

The Many Crossroads of Culture

Antônio Alves Teixeira in his book on Pomba Gira, published in an inferior and reduced English translation in 1990 with his most important introductory chapters discarded, presents a Hermetic model for understanding Genesis in light of Quimbanda. As expected our brother in Faith uses the account in Genesis 1:26 and 27 where it is said that men and women were created in God's image. He sees the transition of new Pomba Giras as a mysterious transmigration where a woman that holds a particular affinity with the realm of emotion and knows the tyranny of macho-men can turn into a Pomba Gira upon death. I believe this is why he sees Exu Woman (Pomba Gira) as being the wife of Exu Calunga (Syrach) as this Exu is the holder of ancestral memory that lives on in the abysmal waters. There is a strong Kongolese legacy of perceiving memory equated with water. Water is also linked to rebirth, hence the graveyard becomes the little Calunga. Alves also continues the idea set forth by Aluizio Fontenelle in the book he penned about Exu in the late 40s, where we find the syncretism with goetic spirits. I am aware that the syncretism with Quimbanda is from the *Grimorium Verum*, but I understand goetic as a denomination for a necromantic tradition reflected in several grammars of nigromancy. This larger goetic scope is also evident in more recent attempts at including Exus that fell outside of the syncretism with *Verum* spirits and have been given demonic veils from other grimoires. This matter deserves further explanation.

Exu Calunga was seen as sharing affinities with Syrach by Fontenelle. Syrach is said to be a duke, meaning he is of the nature of Venus, which is the celestial point for the powers of Pomba Gira. He is also called Gnomo in some sources. At first I could not make much sense of this description of Exu Calunga as a gnome or a leprechaun type of spirit. Only after presenting this issue to the dream vessel did matters become clear. He appeared as a giant hunchback swirling in liquid space. But rather than staying in this Quasimodo-like form, the spirit took the shape of a Byronesque figure, quite intriguing as Byron was reputed not only to be beautiful but to have suffered from a deformed foot. From this perspective it became quite clear what form of intermediary between space and the stars and waters and memory he represents. We see this in many representations of Exu where he has one cloven hoof and one human foot. This sheds light on Jake Stratton-Kent's studies concerning Scirlin's role in *Grimorium Verum* (*The True Grimoire* 2009). This further suggests that the assimilation between the goetic spirits and the retinue of Quimbanda was no accident, but that there is indeed a shared affinity that goes deeper than a mere syncretistic activity motivated by the immediate similarities.

This mystery gains further depth in one of the aliases of Exu Calunga, Exu Cainana. Cainana is a snake that transgresses all kingdoms and can be found with as great an ease in waters and trees as in open spaces and the wilderness. It is never far from water and resonates with the descriptions of kisimbi. It is the serpentine motion that goes through Pomba Gira's spine and structure. There are a great number of myths connected to this snake which links this creature to the protector of the forest, usually depicted as a deformed man of small stature, a gnome. Amongst the Iroquois this spirit is called Hadui and is associated with the strong winds of winter who gives healing and sickness and lives in the tobacco. Similar qualities are given to the helper of the Yorubá Osanyin, lord of the forest, in the shape of his short, dog-headed helper, Aroni. Aroni is said to abduct children that are marked for the patronage of Osanyin and is equally associated with cold winds and thunder as much as the withering of leaves in his role as an intermediary and messenger between the wild and the world of humans. If we add to this that the legend of Osanyin is that he was a star in nature similar to Venus who fell to earth in the city of Irawo, meaning *star* in Yorubá, we have marked the crossroad of Exu Calunga. From his fall all vegetation was made possible and thus through this we find a formula of Venus in her subterrestrial transformation as beauty marked by a physiological deformity pertaining to the night of the woods and the underworld. Her beauty lives on in plants, she is the fertility of a chosen kingdom.

Exu Calunga/Syrach

Pomba Gira/Klepoth

Pomba Gira is only given one spirit in the syncretism with *Grimorium Verum*, and that is Klepoth. Quite interestingly, Klepoth is also a kingdom and not solely an individual spirit, which is quite proper given Pomba Gira's inherent dynamic. While all Exus are given a specific spirit, Pomba Gira is given a kingdom and a mystery. She is a world of husks, shells and broken lights. If we look at the seal *Verum* gives for Klepoth we find a distinct serpentine maze presented, and this is also found in several of her pontos riscados as details around her fork. In this we can see why she is one – but many. In Pomba Gira the idea of being legion becomes reality inviting a richness of spiritual denizens that are both unborn and undead.

Rabbinical lore, and in particular the *Zohar* details the Sitra Ahra, the 'other world'. It is here we find the klepoths, broken kernels of light, born from an excess found at the left side of the Tree of Life, where the powers of severity reside. The world of shells resonates with the material world and some even think there is little difference between the world of klipoth and the material world, known as Assiah. Hell is here in the world of matter, but beneath our feet its roots rest. The klipoth can be elemental spirits but they can also be the husks of dead human beings, that is, passionate memories sustaining some form of personality, as well as being quite benevolent and upright. It is a reflection of the human world. In a way we are caught between two mirrors or more properly, two inverse pyramids. The meeting between the two peaks manifests our world.

Samael and Lilith are the rulers of the Sitra Ahra and consequently there have been some attempts at a direct syncretism between Samael and Lilith and Exu Rei and Pomba Gira Rainha. I find this correlation to be complicated in many ways. One is the discrepancy set forth in this book and the rabbinical doctrines concerning Sitra Ahra which raises the issue of defining the location and nature of the other side versus the underworld. It also questions the importance of ancestral memory, which is crucial in Quimbanda, situating them in a quite different position in the creative design of cosmic necessity. It is better to see this connection as a recognition of shared frequency with the potencies of severity, though operating under different conditions. An important factor in the mystery of Sitra Ahra, is that the other world is seen as being kept alive by human transgression and sin. In other words, the greater the distortions in the material world the stronger 'the other side' is.

Queen Pomba Gira has also been identified with Hecate. They do share the triple crossroad, but there are too many discrepancies involved to make a direct link, even if they do provide mutual clarification. Whilst there are similarities, we should not identify one as the other. It is, as discussed earlier, a refrain that plays out in countless manifestations of blood and passion at the crossroads. The collective form of this potency is called Pagan Pomba Gira, and if we wish to understand Hecate as a Pomba Gira it is to this force we must turn our attention.

Pomba Gira Pagã can refer to any spirit in the line of the Orient, meaning a Pomba Gira of non-Catholic denomination. This encompasses a myriad of spirits which are well versed in the works of separation and rupture. That they are pagan does not necessarily mean they are wild and untamed. However, all Pomba Giras that are pagan are reputed to be cunning in discovering the paternity of children and seem to take an interest in infants in a manner akin to midwives. It is also a common feature of these spirits to be fond of pork and milk. This is a most uncanny offering if we remember that some of these spirits would have a Muslim origin. This offering gives purity and impurity in equal amounts and some sort of wicked equilibrium is attained.

Ponto Cantado of Pomba Gira Pagã

Ela não foi batizada	*She was never baptized*
Não buscou a salvação (*bis*)	*Never searching for salvation* (× 2)
Mas è aquele quem vence demanda	*But it is She that wins the demand*
Saravá Pomba Gira Pagã (*bis*)	*Saravá Pomba Gira Pagan* (× 2)

Ponto Riscado of Pomba Gira Pagã

This ponto is used in most workings, and gives great stability to them, and to any incorporation of spirit. But the ponto is also quite revealing of the nature of these spirits. The reaper cuts off the force of Pomba Gira at the root and she is enabled to ascend upwards. In her case, as a denizen of the underworld she will rise to the material world. The umbilical cord of the dead is severed and a new function can occur, regulated in accordance with an outlandish design of evolution. It is from this point onwards that the spirit can become more evolved through healthy attachments to humans and can be baptized. This simply refers to entering a spiritual adolescence that gives way to being crowned upon becoming an adult. We can not understand this in relation to human gestation and maturation, there are other laws ruling this process which are largely forgotten but have curiously resurfaced in modern vampire tales. The newly turned goes through a wild phase until reaching stability and equilibrium. It is maturation in a new state of being. But fear not, I shall not resort to popular television series and Hollywood to deepen this, rather I shall call upon the works of Claude Lecouteux.

Lecouteux roots his research in parallels between Roman and Scandinavian history. He deepens our understanding of what happens with a mystery such as death in the transition from a traditional to a profane world view. He reminds us that in Rome the deceased were shunned because they were potentially dangerous. Why were the dead a subject for fear? Because after all, they were dead. Just the presence of fear related to death shows how easy it is for moderns to misunderstand how people used to see the dead. Today with our lack of awareness of the dead as ancestors, and the Church's insistence on moving the dead away from their dwellings and farms to cemeteries, we understand death differently – and the dead accordingly act differently. In the past when the dead were buried in their land, rites of burial and the proper preparation of the grave done, the dead were literally seated beneath the earth and continued to influence the living in vision and dreams. When in the early Middle Ages the Church outlawed this custom and threw the poor into mass graves they also generated host upon host of rootless and restless dead. In Quimbanda we make a pleasant abode for the dislocated dead one, so we can partake of their ancestral knowledge. A rectification of this loss of ancestry still makes part of genuine lineages of Quimbanda, where the bones of a given Tatá are reanimated. They are placed in a spirit jar where they can dwell and continue to exert their influence.

In ancient Rome the dead were seen as the cause of much misfortune and also of possession. A person possessed by the dead was said to be a *larvætus*. The larvæ were commonly understood to be the hostile dead, those who died in agony or as a result of crimes. As Ovid tells us in *Fasti*, the custom of annual placation of the dead ceased and its results were sterility of the womb, epilepsy and various states of possession we today deem insanity. The feast called Parentalia was introduced to end these misfortunes and thus all the dead were included in the notion of parentage and ancestry. From this it is clear that the dead continued to influence the living because they were still vigorous in their transformed state. The importance of funeral rites has always been to give the dead rest. All funerary rites are exorcisms and appeasements of the departed. This is, at least, the conclusion we draw from Roman laws that prohibited any transition of the departed's estate until the funeral rites had been carried out correctly. Lecouteux informs us that: *Criminals had no right to a ritual burial. Their bodies were tossed upon Esquiline field, where, as Horace tells us, the witches would go at sunset to collect ingredients for their potions.* (Lecouteux 2009:15). These are the restless dead, troublesome revenants that refuse to conform to the natural law. These departed souls who resist dissipation and instead linger on to create trouble or bring solace are a contradiction, neither here nor there, but move between being and death, presence and silence.

If we recall Norse mythology, the dead had many options. They could go to Valhalla, to Ran's kingdom beneath the sea or to the halls of Hel. What this tells us is that there was definitively a state of being once life on earth was done with. But what if these three options are closed doors and one must linger on in the in-between? As we read in the 11th century German poem *Summa Theologica*, the dead never cease to be, they simply transform into earth: our flesh, dew, our sweat, stones, our bones, plants, our veins, grass, our hair and fluids, our blood. They simply rise in the kingdoms of nature – and as our world moves on in our illusion of progress, new kingdoms are made, or recognised, such as those of the tavern and brothel.

What is intriguing in this imagery is that we can never escape the dead. They find their place no matter whether we turn aside or recoil. If we step on land and earth we are stepping on the veil that separates us from our ancestors. So death is what connects us not only to ancestry, but to memory. It is this memory, that once had a family but is now dispersed over the earth, which Quimbanda gathers, and herein is its beauty and danger. The beauty lies in the rescuing of lost souls from the sands of forgotten memory, and here we also find its danger.

In accounts we have of the restless dead, they often bring trouble in an attempt to direct our attention back to them. When they do this it is because they have found a substitute home. They make themselves known because they smell a connection, a memory that flows like mud between the worlds. In this we find their taste for earth, liquids and plants as this is the essence of death. Quimbandeiros are not really doing anything different from the 11th century poem, but are taking it literally, a fresh vibrant grave is made for the spirit to reside within.

This is telling, insofar as the force and memory of the dead as blood or spiritual ancestors are brought to life. This explains why spirit vessels are comforting homes for a spirit to rest and work from. The quimbandeiro when he goes to the cemetery to buy a soul is not buying one that has, but one that seeks, comfort. He or she is buying a soul that has not found rest and thus chance enters. Will you treat this wild and forlorn soul as a slave or as a friend? The spirit will evolve and gain strength both by prayers, petition, blood, force and memory. When the spirit gains both power and direction, what then? Have you made a friend or created a rebellious slave?

These motives are important for our lives, they are mirrors, and in this I would like to present a vision, born by spirit, that can benefit all humans and in particular women.

Pomba Gira in the Mirror of Female Evolution

For women, and perhaps modern woman in particular, Pomba Gira can be a tremendous inspiration and a source for understanding womanhood itself. It is customary in Quimbanda to understand spirit undergoing an evolution from pagan to crowned. Commonly, this is given Christian qualities, but is in reality an expression of the maturation of the returning dead. We enter the world pagan, meaning wild and unrestrained; in the course of life we reach adolescence, paralleled by the baptised spirit; when adolescence gives way to maturity and self-knowledge they are crowned. The same sequence is also reflected in the transition of Pomba Gira.

We find in the sphere of pagan activity Pomba Gira Menina (Pomba Gira Girl) and Pomba Gira Pagã, as the powers that constitute the female substance from which she will grow. We find in these two forms the dyadic relationship between the sweet and the more unrestrained child, the pleaser and the explorer.

At adolescence/baptism this orientation takes form in Pomba Gira Cigana and the various Pomba Giras of the kingdom of the Lyre and Streets. A world of possibility where womanhood can shine opens up, and by working with these forms of Pomba Gira a deeper understanding of adolescence can be gained. Frequently in this phase, encounters with Pomba Gira das Sete Encruzilhadas (Seven Crossroads) happen. The understanding you enter with here will generate your choices. These meetings typify a given direction which we find in Pomba Gira Rainha das Sete Cruzes, Maria Molambo and Pomba Gira Rainha das Almas. This triplicity is concerned with nurture/solace (das Almas/Souls), protection/defense (Sete Cruzes/Seven Crosses) and presence/expansion (Molambo).

Depending on affinity, woman now enters the kingdoms of Praia (beach) or Calunga where a maturation of emotions and self-image transpires. Woman chooses between the depth of the waters or its surface. The woman who gravitates towards an easy-going and fun-loving life has chosen the beach. Calunga opens to those for whom this is unsatisfactory and who seek challenges.

The crowning process is completed when woman becomes self-assertive and free from guilt. This is enabled by Pomba Gira Dama da Noite (Lady of the Night) which leads to the crown itself, Rainha Maria Padilha as she is moved by Maria Padilha da Figueira do Inferno, into a unique manifestation. Some women can embrace the Queen of the Fig Tree, a rare but astonishing feat. She returns to a point of origin and unique being where the pivotal tree of fire is mastered.

The various stages and transitions reveal themselves when woman ceases to need the counsel of her Pomba Gira. This marks a transition where new challenges and different needs manifest.

A known Pomba Gira can resonate in distinct ways when reacting with the bio energetic patterns and passions of the medium. This might explain why some possessions initially give the impression of being doubtful. That is, until the messages are presented. In these cases there is a merging between spirit and the energetic currents of the medium, a marvelous occurence where the veil between votary and spirit is broken.

This transformative quality, akin to evolution, is explained if we understand these spirits to be ontologically similar to Di Manes, in life so in death the potential for maturation occurs.

Pomba Gira Sete Maridos (Seven Husbands) is an alternative name for Pomba Gira Sete Porteiras which reveals her as a spirit that always finds a way. She is also unpredictable, for we cannot know which door she will open, or what husband she will send out, to effectuate her work. The ways she chooses to accomplish a demand or request are important to understand. While we may see a natural development towards the solution in one way, she perceives it in multiple ways. This in itself can confuse us when we witness her working: our anticipation, and her play on our insecurities, comprise in part the solution.

Pomba Gira as the woman of seven husbands reveals her as the source of power in Quimbanda. However, there is also the question of ownership. On a practical level, any man a woman has demanded from her is never her property, the male gift is always borrowed from Pomba Gira. There is a price involved and rigid observation of her cult, or at the very least your promise and word, is needed in order for her gift to endure. She will never hand you the object of your desire without engaging in teaching you. Foolish requests might manifest as well as clever ones, and whether you have requested a curse or a blessing, responsibility ultimately falls upon you. You have what you have been given for as long as you respectfully acknowledge the source of the gift. This goes for gifts you realised were not really what you wanted, as well as for blessings bestowed.

Pomba Gira attaches herself most favorably to men in spells of love, whilst using her to affect a woman's sentiments seems to be less speedy than using her in seductive works targeting the man. When she is sent to a woman and attempts her seduction, dreams start and strange situations occur that bring her attention upon the lusting man. The process can take time as she does not work on women's passion in the same way as she does with men. With women she softly seduces the attention, while in men she inflames sexual arousal. Women subject to her powers are treated with greater understanding and often more tenderly than she would treat a man. Because of this intricate web of seduction and passion, I have come to be careful with bindings and rarely agree to bind what should be free. Exceptions to this rule are cases where works of separation have been applied. We are then faced with a different degree of complexity where tying and untying must be done.

She plays on the vile and seductive to facilitate growth. Just as these spirits evolve from pagan to baptised and finally receive a crown, so too do we. In our meetings with them time is often important to cultivate and nurture a genuine connection. This works best if we approach the connection out of love for the spirit herself, and not for the gifts she can give. It is advisable to pay reverence to the Queens as they are more stable, whatever your state of spiritual evolution. If you undertake a working full of anger and resentment, and treat her as the means for a selfish solution, you can be sure that your own 'pagan' disposition will tempt the same response out, even from a Queen. A Queen will teach you to master wild passions so you can be like her, both mature and perceptive. By extension this means that a mature person can work with younger and more 'pagan' spirits with greater benefits than the juvenile and power hungry votary.

When I first began to practice this cult I had some unexpected results and some workings failed, or so I thought. Only later, as I matured in my understanding of Pomba Gira, did I see that the working was actually acomplished, but in highly unexpected ways. She had worked on me so that the opportunities for my desire would arise – but absorbed in contemplating why the ritual did not work I missed my opportunities. This happened several times until I got it and realised that she is the crossroad of perpetual chance!

The door to her mystery starts with a Pomba Gira called Sete Gargalhadas, the Seven Laughs. As you commence working with her, this is the Pomba Gira that you will hear most often. The carefree, humbling laugh of something terrifying that wants to mock you – or so you believe. This is a healthy beginning and a sign that she has taken a positive interest in you. Her laughter is the joy of life, it is a message to us to dive into the world with awareness and joy, no matter what comes. As she teaches you about the beauty of the rose, she also reminds you of its thorns. The path of challenges opens up as you are slowly roasted on her rejuvenating fire. Men especially find this challenging, as she will cause an arrogant chauvinist to be humbled and ridiculed in enigmatic ways before she gives her wisdom. Until that realisation, wishes may come true yet always with a price. It falls to you to grasp that this tortuous road is the waymark of a rewarding relationship with her.

The Seat of Vanity

Pomba Gira represents the principle of vanity and is drawn towards beauty in all forms, this also means that she is simple in her tastes and seeks only the best. This focus on what we understand as vice is important, because the Pomba Giras teach by challenging our vices and false judgments. Thus, she embraces and shamelessly celebrates the absence of guilt. Her vanity is a mask for her inner beauty. Only by coming to terms with the exterior will we be invited inside as allied and trusted companions.

In order to ensure stability in your work with her it is common to erect a tronco or tronceira, which we can understand as a seat of power. This is something any person of virtue and sound reason can undertake. The tronco is essentially a small house, maybe half meter or so in height, that is placed to the left of the door, looking from the outside. This house can be made of a variety of materials and will be painted red inside and black and/or white outside. When working with the tronco decide which day brings the line you seek to work within, and always light a white candle in honour of the line, presenting a glass of high proof alcohol at the foot of the candle. Upon completing the painting you will wash the house in alcohol and burn a seven day candle in front of it until you next choose a day that resonates with the line you have appointed. Now take an image of Pomba Gira and one of Exu and wash them in alcohol and anoint them with a little palm oil and red wine. Take two forks, one for each and do the same. Place them inside the house together with the hair of a mature coconut, star anis and dry red peppers which you also place inside, leaving the offerings in front of Exu and Pomba Gira. Finally bring two virgin glasses and two virgin candleholders, one for each. You will then inaugurate the tronco with a bottle of cachaça, vodka, rum or similar and a bottle of sparkling wine as well as cigarillos and cigars. At this point you will not demand anything. This is your gift and in this moment you have created sacred space. At the inauguration you simply sit and listen, follow your inspiration as they move you to spontaneous song and prayer, but do not make requests and demands. The purpose of the tronco is essentially to give the medium stability in work with the spirit. The tronco wards off intrusive spirits and spirit pretenders and is your security in your future work with Pomba Gira. For the first month, present yourself in front of your tronco every week, on the same day and do the same thing; seven weeks in all shall pass from the painting of the house until your vigil is considered done. This will allow your vibration and theirs to harmonise and you give them a chance to 'sniff you out' and see who you are. By doing this diligently in the prescribed manner you are also showing determination and devotion, and this will in itself call upon the benevolence of the spirits.

When you start to work with them follow a simple procedure: open your sessions by stamping your left foot on the ground three times, then knock with the left fist, saying:

Salve povo de Arruanda
Salve Exu
Salve Pomba Gira
Salve povo de Quimbanda
Laroyé!

Spray the tronco in alcohol, light candles and pour offerings in the glasses. Elect a proper ponto and sing until you feel the presence rising. In this state you can stay in communion with the spirits, meaning you share tobacco and alcohol, or you can request a work.

It is possible to use an oracle outside of the mediumistic activity, such as cards, shells and bones. This is outside the scope of what should be done on a solitary basis, so I suggest that you approach this as a training ground for developing your mediumship and seek confirmation of the results of your communion or work through the dreaming vessel – or apply an oracle upon the finished session as a tool to confirm if you got things right. One possibility is to use a pendulum. Wash it in cachaça and ask yes and no questions, this should safeguard you from errors of perception and understanding.

You will end the session in the same way as you began, leaving the candles to burn out by themselves, stamp three times, state your gratitude and leave taking three steps backwards and then turn around. This is sufficient to mark the beginning and end of a session.

Sometimes we can feel that spirit is not letting go, and even after closing they are still with us. This is not uncommon and can be expected, the boundaries you define will become more stable with time. In the beginning they do tend to flow outside the desired limits, the power of obsession always walks with them. If this happens, cover the tronco with a black veil and take a shower or bath, preferably in herbs like rue and leaves of ginger and wild saffron. If this is not possible, use oil of eucalyptus and cedar either in the bath water or in a body lotion which will have a grounding effect.

As a precaution in your initial work with her watch your vices, in particular in the realm of passion. She will constantly challenge your character here. This is their way of letting us in. We should evaluate our connection with them constantly in the beginning so we are not allowing space for fantasy to take shape through our passions. This also influences the pacts and concords we make with her. And even here she can often challenge the practitioner as he or she takes the first steps. I am here speaking of all factors that gave 'the devil' such a bad reputation – so be cautious and conscious about what you are doing and why – and avoid blaming spirit for your choices. At times, workings take shape in unexpected ways and if we pay attention she reveals the full picture of the situation in unexpected workings – a lesson and a divination takes place and its outcome is mediated by us and our comprehension and ability to follow the flow.

Westerners have learned to fear possession, because in this state we believe we lose control over the social creation we like to call self. We should not fear possession, if anything it expands our being. When she comes down into our body we will first feel a pressure, an intensity that fills us from the centre and then expands out and meets something that erupts from beneath our feet. You will feel compelled to laugh and curse. In the initial stages the possessions tend be quite violent and it is absolutely crucial that you have a trained cambone or similar person, well versed in the dynamics of possession, to safeguard you. A genuine possession will literally take you over. Though in time this violence or crisis will soften, the same sensation of being taken over will be a constant. It is here that the genuine possession takes place, which for some can pave the way for a two-headed possession. This means that spirit allows you to witness it's besiegement of your being. If one has doubts concerning the spirit coming down being the one it declares itself to be, it can be interrogated and one can demand proofs. This is really seldom an issue when a tronco is set up. The trained medium knows instinctively how to bargain with the spirit to resume consciousness again, but a trained assistant is important as someone who guides and controls the possession and decides when it is time to leave. Both spirit and medium work better if they can depend upon the person controlling the possession. A good cambone will represent a natural authority and can by simple request or demand make the spirit leave. Sometimes small concords are enacted, like sealing the promise of leaving by giving the spirit a glass of cachaça or a cigar. Resistant spirits can be expelled with water, preferably cold, as this will quench the fires of hell. It is also possible to place a glass of water containing an egg over the head of the medium and demand with great force and intent that the spirit leaves. I have never witnessed this procedure fail. Over the course of time, the medium and spirit become used to each other and Pomba Gira takes less savage forms and starts to give counsel. When this relationship is established the possession is less severe. There is an initial crisis followed by a dynamic manifestation. The dynamic depends on which Pomba Gira is taking shape. Maria Padilha is usually of a gentler kind, while the Crossroad Pomba Giras are harsh and critical and those of the Lyre and Street often push your limits and boundaries.

The Spirit Book can prove to be a useful tool for having better control over the sessions. By this I mean a consecrated book that you will use to prepare your sessions. Note down the nature of your inquiries and record the responses; evaluate, rephrase and expand until the next session. This can be a good thing, as these spirits tend to be quite talkative when they get going. To prepare yourself and have the book at hand is a good way of monitoring the sessions and getting greater benefit from them. When you start to work with her along these lines, and she accepts your presence in her cult, you will notice an upsurge of enthusiasm, creativity and inspirations of various kinds. Not all of this is necessarily meaningful, as the meaning rests in quickening these faculties, more than what you produce initially. These are additional avenues where she manifests herself. Visions of beauty seen with new eyes are perhaps a reflection born from her and not you. Likewise, she inspires song and poetry – so allow this creative impulse to flow into your life. This is a wonderful way of giving safe and beautiful manifestation to spirit. In this, Pomba Gira shares the ecstatic and creative impulse with the exposition on Babalon, *The Red Goddess*, by Peter Grey (2007). There is a common flame between Pomba Gira and Babalon and for Westerners this discourse might prove useful in providing a canvas upon which we can perceive Pomba Gira. This brings us to a mystery that is not much commented upon, but is an experience I and several others have had, that is, her role as a muse. Such a rapport made between us and spirit is most fortunate, as this is the kind of relationship that abides in love and spiritual inter-est. In Quimbanda proper, this is demonstrated in the relationship one has with one's spirit guide/Tatá/Yayá. When you have your spirit guide confirmed, meaning who your Pomba Gira is, this marks the be-ginning of presence. A friend commented upon this initial stage with Pomba Gira Cigana that she is fiercely protective of anyone who shows bravery in times of difficulty and looks for those with strong hearts. I can't agree more, this is hitting the nail of hell on the head. Here we discover what she gives: the opportunity to solve your own nefarious inclinations by being their mirror. She flies to the brave as any maid approached by a dragon-slaying knight.

We also need to discuss two more factors; one is the complex of obsession, the other the notion of offending the spirits. Let us speak of the latter first. The idea of offending the spirits does not rest in making ritual mistakes as much as it is a product of breaking oaths and being dishonourable. We have to understand that Pomba Gira is the principle of beauty, its virtue so to speak, that has been persecuted over time by malicious people of every denomination and intent. So, you need to approach her respectfully, as a Queen. You approach her because you have appointed her as the one to solve your situation. If you do this, she will receive you as a knight. In the same measure, a man that approaches her as a slut will be treated as a slut. It is also fairly common to present to Pomba Gira a gift when we demand a result and promise an additional gift upon completion – or a multipli-cation of what is already given, often 3, 7 or 9 fold. This promise being made, it must be fulfilled unless you wish to suffer her as a torment in your life that sabotages your relationships and self-esteem. Outside of

this, if you are working the cult without guidance, keep it simple and pay attention to these rules and you shall be fine, no harm shall come to you – only the challenges that will make you a Knight and a Queen.

Obsession is an eternal hazard in the work with Pomba Gira – after all, the passions of the soul are her domain. Obsession is noticed when the world we live in brings ominous inspirations, down to the most insignificant act – or you take on one of her lewd masks in your mundane life and act out a parody of her. At times this can be psychologically healthy, transgressing the boundaries she invites us to break can be good – but we cannot forget to bring our reason with us in this. Obsession is most unhealthy and is a power that breaks and crushes love and relationships, the spirits of obsession are often called kiumbas and are powers of murky, undirected light that feed upon our passions. Thus they act upon them causing us to produce more. Many accounts of 'demonic possessions' are also provoked by these spiritual entities. The kiumbas are understood and applied by Exus in the line of Malei and also by Exus like Morçego (Bat) and Marabó. They are however a potency belonging to Pomba Gira Queen of the Fig Tree in Hell. Obsessions begin with a situation where your mind is taken over by your passions, you cannot think of anything other than her, or the badly-directed petition you made in demanding a working. The sooner we confront this, the better. It may be that these symptoms indicate that you should give Pomba Gira the same offering as you gave her for having the work done, but this time with the request to cancel it. Be humble and for seven weeks do nothing but light a weekly candle in her honour. No sessions, just a weekly token of respect followed by a purifying bath. If we observe these matters we shall walk well in this path and harvest immense benefits.

The Gifts of Vanity and Beauty

As repeatedly stressed, Pomba Gira is the fullness of Woman, and it is important to make her feel like a Queen. It is time to present some general workings that can be used to honour whatever Pomba Gira you seek to know. In many ways to placate Pomba Gira is like going to the house of a harsh but wise and voluptuous mistress. Would you arrive without gifts? Would you go arrogant, or with the intention of seducing her to enjoy your presence, the one you are – even when she questions your very being?

The classic offering is the padé, of which there are many forms. I will give here one formula that will be accepted by all Pomba Giras:

Take a good amount of palm oil and fry it with red onion, fennel seeds and a hand of red chilli peppers. Bring it to a boil and simmer for a few minutes, then blend in coarse corn flour stirring until you have a dry and grainy texture, and blend in cachaça or red wine.

Take an alguidar and place inside a piece of red silk or velvet and place the dish inside. You then decorate the dish with 21 chilli peppers and 21 cowries, pouring a generous amount of honey over it. This is a simple padé that can be offered to any Pomba Gira as a gift or as a part of a demand/request.

She is also fond of perfumes. Purchase sweet smelling perfumes, or just as good, make infusions or oils. I tend to prefer oils as this is a good medium for consecration in general and I find presence to be better stored in this medium. A simple and marvelous Pomba Gira oil can be made in the following way:

You will at nightfall on a Friday, preferably close to the full moon, go to three kingdoms: the Lyre, the street and the wilderness. You will in each of these kingdoms search out a crossroad and take from there a pinch of earth, leaving a coin and a cigarette in exchange. Bring this before your tronco, light a candle for Pomba Gira and open a session. Have a cup of virgin olive oil with you, a good quality essence of cassia, anis and roses, three drops of each. Now doing this you will add to the oil three more drops of the scent you require to call upon Pomba Gira. Use rose if you want to call upon her for love and fun, cassia if you seek her more mature and demanding forms, and anis if you want her to walk with you as a muse. You will then add the earth you took and leave it in your tronco at the foot of Pomba Gira, ensuring candles are burning until daybreak. The next day – and this is important – you will at midnight give her a cigarillo and a glass of red wine. Give this with your left hand as you take the oil with your right. Anoint her with the oil and anoint yourself wisely.

Of beverages she always takes champagne, cachaça and many Queens take whiskey. If you have these drinks available together with anisette you should have offerings ready for any occasion. Remember that these spirits grow stronger in alcohol and tobacco and the types of alcohol used can at times influence the type of presence she emanates. This means that whiskey typically tends to solidify the manifestation of a Queen, the smokiness of the whiskey bringing forth her more brutal core, while champagne brings out a more benevolent aspect, like the anisette. The cachaça is good to use, the sugarcane is a wonderful base for spirit manifestation. Some Pomba Giras also take absinthe and chartreuse, though it is better not to give them the taste of this too early; these offerings belong more to the line of Malei to provoke negative aspects of the spirits. In a way, always use yourself as a measure, because these spirits respond to your biocircuitry and state of mind and passions. It is a union as close to the veil of the other as we can get, and we need to appraise and appreciate our connection in light of this. Quimbanda brings the dead and undead to life, we are the medium they use for their manifestation, thus bad intentions give a bad direction, as much as good intentions give a good direction. In this we find the core of the Kardec/Umbanda idea of the spirits of Quimbanda being in need of evolution, often mistaking the mirroring as part of their mystery. This at least is my experience and understanding. This also places the spirits in a position where they can guide us, and we can also guide them. It is a wicked equality suggestive of a balance between the dead and the living as we all approach the veil.

93

Pomba Gira is captivating and enigmatic, mesmerising and attractive, and at the same time unpredictable, kind, severe – above all, she escapes definition even as one attempts to encircle her domain and nature. The perception of Pomba Gira varies from seeing her as a divine whore to a not-so-divine whore. She is rather the infernal lover of the Devil, seen as representing the dark side of spirituality, the left hand of Umbanda. She is also found in some houses of Catimbó and in Candomblé, especially the houses of Angola, given her relationship to the Congolese mysteries.

She has been attributed to a spirit called Bongbongira and also Pambunjila, Mavambu and Aluvaia, as this deity is found amongst many Bantu speaking people and accordingly coloured by different dialects. One can also assume that the name Bongbongira is a contraction and alteration of *mpungo* and *nzila* which means *spirit of the road* and gives a nuance to what has been revealed earlier in the text as it insists on the importance of the street and not the crossroads. In present day Brazil, the name Pomba Gira means literally *dove that flies around* and has a somewhat sweet connotation that relates this spirit to divine grace and the holy spirit and the whole series of mysteries mirrored in the functions of Salomé, Martha and Mary Magdalene. These connotations have never before been mentioned in relation to Pomba Gira, as the interpretation of this spirit is usually done from the perspective of Umbandistas, which gives her the role of the devil's Congolese wife. The legions of Pomba Gira became in time a shorthand for witchy women of European origin, like the most famous and beloved of the Pomba Giras, Maria Padilha. The European influence on the practice of Quimbanda seeped in during the 1920s with the rise of Umbanda, and consequently there was a merging of the cultivation of Exu with Umbanda under the name of Quimbanda.

In the present day, Quimbanda is seen as the left hand of Umbanda, as the negative pole of the positive syncretism within the spiritism of Umbanda. Some attempts have been made to revitalise parts of the cult on a European basis, like the syncretism between Exus and the demonic spirits of *Grimorium Verum* in the late 50s and the appearance of Exu Belzebuth in the shape of Baphomet in the mid 70s. This suggests that spirit has tried all along to remind us about this forgotten heritage of Quimbanda. In the modern day, the awareness of Pomba Gira's origin and the European heritage of Quimbanda has entered into the awareness of practitioners. This is demonstrated in the research of Laura de Mello e Souza and Marlyse Meyer. An inferior presentation has been given in the popular book by Maria Helena Farelli, who in her depiction of the witches of Evora and the Iberian conjurations of Maria Padilha, popularised the research of Meyer and Souza, presenting Pomba Gira as an archetypical witch. This is quite acceptable and in harmony with the essence of this book. She never limits herself unless we do.

Syncretism of Pomba Gira with obscure global demonesses has also been attempted. What I find interesting in this list is that these female 'demons' are not only obscure, but all they have in common is that they are vile, dangerous and many are very close to the mystery of succubæ. The list is as follows:

Rainha das 7 Encruzilhadas	Astartea
Rainha 7 Cruzeiros	Pitits
Rainha da Calunga Pequena	Lilith
Rainha das Almas	Allatou
Rainha das Matas	Proserpina
Rainha da Praia	Klepoth
Pomba Gira Cigana	Mara
Pomba Gira Maria Mulambo	Aluca
Pomba Gira Rosa Caveira	Baalberith
Pomba Gira da Kalunga	Lamastu
Pomba Gira Maria Quitéria	Lamia

Pomba Gira das Cobras	Nagini
Pomba Gira Dama da Noite	Noctiluca
Pomba Gira das Almas	Rusalkis
Pomba Gira da Praia	Iset Zemunin
Pomba Gira do Luar	Upierzyca
Pomba Gira Menina	Viechtitsa
Pomba Gira do Sol	Keteb

I do not intend to discuss these matters and their discrepancies, beyond stating the connection they have with vampirism and witchcraft. Personally I find most of these aliases to be puzzling and I cannot really see the dots that connect demoness and Pomba Gira. What I find important however, is the relationship all of these succubæ have with wind, coldness and night. This will place them in the status of potential familiars seen from a European Craft perspective, or as matrons of certain witch mysteries that call upon the attention of spirit guides and various other denizens that gravitate towards humans. This European connection has been downplayed in recent years, but continues in the form of Maria Padilha.

The most famous conjuration of Maria Padilha is the one collected by the Holy Office in Valencia in 1655, reproduced in the research of Souza, and Meyer. It is possible, though not frequent, to find fragments of this used in terreiros all over Brazil. The working is simple, and as follows:

I conjure NN
By Barrabás
By Satanás
By the limp Devil
Who can do more

(The request is done)

By the wife of Satanás
By the wife of Barrabás
By the wife of Belzebub

(The working is performed)

By Barrabás, by Satanás and Lucifer
By the Lady Maria Padilha
And her legions

(The ritual is sealed up)

We find this triad in the three lines of command, the three generals of the maioral. These three generals are Exu Lucifer, Exu Mor/Belzebub and Exu King of Seven Crossroads/Ashtaroth. These are the 'husbands' of Maria Padilha, who is revealed to be the one that is actually controlling the legions. It is clear in the spell that the appeal is given to her, which she then communicates to her kings.

She is Exu Woman, she holds all that Exu has, and more besides. She is Exu combined with sweet aromas and vibrant waters. Some common perspectives upon Pomba Gira are rooted in a good/evil dichotomy and draped in the clothes of divine opposition. This idea is simply not correct. Rather we can perceive Exu and Pomba Gira as King and Queen of our lower soul, that is, the world of passions and emotions. Ideally the world of passion should be obedient to the world of reason, so the higher moves the lower. In this way we enable ourselves to gain a greater perspective upon life and to make better choices. In this we find the secret that makes mastery and slavery.

Those drawn to these spirits, desiring to work with them on the premise that they are demons and devils, and motivated by an appetite for some perceived dark power, should be careful. Since these spirits return what you are, it is important to be honest about one's reason for working. If a darker approach is only sought to cover up an inferiority complex or fear, this will at some point come back to haunt you.

97

Accepting their threshold position as Kings and Queens of the lower soul, they will naturally be fed by emotions, anger and turbulence.

Their unruly nature probably led to the notion amongst Umbandistas of placing the Exus as servants of Orixás. In seeing the darkness as the servant for the light, the evolutionary theories of Kardec also entered the picture. As a consequence of the idea of evolution, these spirits were restricted to being seen as potencies which could be enlightened by doing God's work.

Everybody has an Exu and a Pomba Gira, given that passion is a part of the human condition. We should also note that the male/female distinction at its most fundamental level represents the capacity of force and aggression in the form of Exu, and emotional and sexual dominance in the form of Pomba Gira. Additions to the legions of Exu are commonly from the male representatives of humans, and for Pomba Gira female, though on an energetic level, from the soul. Accordingly we ascribe the understanding of femaleness to matters of the heart and emotions while aggression is attributed to maleness. It is in the mastery of one's passions that one can define who is master and who is slave in this spiritual relationship.

Working with these spirits requires that you know yourself well, because they will test you and force you towards self knowledge. Any perversion, any clandestine secret that the dark of the moon is hiding, is bound to surface if you seek out Pomba Gira's help and friendship. Another mistake is to see her as a prostitute. If you approach her as a prostitute this is the face she will show and accordingly, she will charge you handsomely and challenge this idea, often in cruel ways. She does not give a second thought to taking you as far as she deems necessary for you to understand her.

The ultimate lesson of Pomba Gira is the respect and understanding of womanhood. This can happen both by challenging ridiculous perspectives, and also by taking an interest in her people. Sometimes you can hear it commented that such and such a person has *Pomba Gira in front*. This means that for some votaries, Pomba Gira takes the lead in that person's life. This is good for the person in question, as the essence of Woman is constant. Yet, this also causes those around to notice the Pomba Gira first and react to this. People that have Pomba Gira in front will constantly be met with challenges and even potentially dangerous situations; this will be ongoing until the power is taken back and the spine fortified by these experiences.

Obsessive workings with Pomba Gira based on a vulgar conception of her identity as a prostitute and a slave we can command to do our bidding, as long as we seduce her with gifts and offerings, is not recommended. It will certainly produce unpredictable results and sometimes she can even infect one's sexual current. There are examples of men who found themselves increasingly obsessed with same-sex fantasies, and women who developed a curiosity for prostitution that was only quenched by trying it. When this happens, things have gone too far and it is important to mention this, as obsession is often a sign that something is not right.

Another common mistake is to place unreasonable demands on spirit and also ask for assistance in areas where the power in question has little influence. For instance, to ask Pomba Gira Rainha das Sete Encruzilhadas to solve one's emotional turmoil is perhaps not the best idea, unless this is one's personal Pomba Gira. One would be better advised to turn to Pomba Gira da Praia to solve such issues. Misplaced and unreasonable demands generate frustration between you and the spirit. One should be aware that Pomba Gira is not an easy spirit and the practitioner needs to invest much time and energy in establishing a good relationship with her. This involves giving attention to one's passionate world and lower aspirations.

Contrary to popular belief, most of these spirits do not revel in delight when they are sent to do mischief. The delight places demands on the relationship the spirit has with its Tatá or Yayá. Works done by people of good heart and generous soul are more often rewarded than works done by sinister people approaching Pomba Gira as their servant. A sense of justice is at work amongst these legions. Their justice is not tied to morality and ethics, as we understand them. Rather, it is a question of communion and clanship. If we work these spirits out of love for the spirits themselves, they provide protection and defence automatically. If we remain aloof from our raging passions, so will

they, which also has consequences for their sense of justice. Quite simply, if someone picks on one of the clan members, the spirits will not hesitate to give the culprit a lesson. The more calm our soul is, the more refined is the work of these spirits.

In order to work with Pomba Gira we need to offer to her materials that are on her frequency: objects from the mineral, vegetable and animal kingdom that resonate with her energetic presence. Accordingly such offerings both manifest the spirit in the sacred space, and give the spirit the fuel to carry out the request. The items used in workings for Pomba Gira are *pemba* (chalk) in white, red and black, ribbons and candles in the same colours, champagne, cigarillos or cigarettes, matches, fine china and crystal, jewelry, silk cloth, olive oil, palm oil, essential oils, lipstick, make up, combs, red roses (usually without thorns), eggs, graveyard dust, various precious stones and metals. The workings are preferably done in places of power, the natural sites such as crossroad, cemetery, beach or the woods. Alternatively, one can make the workings in the terreiro of Pomba Gira and give the offering at the crossroad. How this works in practice will be made evident in the spirit catalogue.

Usually the effects desired will take some time to manifest, as time is a wicked issue for her. A work will often give results after a few days, but depending on the nature of the working itself, they can be delayed for weeks or months – though the desire usually manifests within one lunar cycle. The lunar cycle should be observed when working with Pomba Gira. The new moon is elected for bindings and prosperity workings, a waning moon for harmful workings, and a waxing moon for workings of growth. Hence, a spell for binding is better performed in the last three days of the moon's waning towards the new moon, while a spell to secure emotional love is better performed under the light of the full moon. The hour most frequently chosen is the Great Hour, meaning midnight. It is when the moon rises that the kingdom of Quimbanda awakens, and both the midnight of Venus and midnight proper can be used as peak hours.

THE IDEA OF KINGDOMS has gone through a cultural forgetting, hand in hand with a resurgence in various cults. Though its contemporary form was established with Umbanda, it is necessary to suggest some avenues of development to demonstrate how dynamic and vibrant Quimbanda is Let us take *das Almas*, or *of the Souls*, given as a quality to many Exus and Pomba Giras. This quality reveals a preoccupation with the transmigration of souls and the mysteries of death and consciousness. We see this in the *guias* whose white beads reveals a connection with *das Almas*. This quality is often worked at the Cruzerio, the central Cross in the boneyard, that serves as the axis of ascent for souls. Most people will claim that this quality was introduced into Umbanda by Kardecism. Whilst this is true, it might also be true that the root goes deeper. There is yet another line, called Moussorubi, which is at root related to the Malê, Muslims from the area of Mali and Sudan that were particularly represented in the state of Alagoas. These people were also called Malinka and Madinga, and this referred to those Africans who were neither Bantu nor Yorubá. The Yorubás were known by the generic Nagô. What is clear from the reports available is that these Madingas were not Muslims in the strict sense, as they also made cult to meteorites and thunderstones and the deities associated with them. The Malê people shared much in common with the Yorubás but their reputation was nefarious with stories of djinn and demons attached to them. Curiously, a similar reputation to the Yorubá holds for the Fulani people found in the more central areas of South West Africa, who are feared, respected and shunned due to their potent herbal knowledge and ability to control the djinn for malefic ends. Protasius Frikel speaks of how the Gêgê and Nagô people are different from the Malê in respect to death. He calls the Malê *dead ones* and points out that they keep houses for the dead and attend to them with diligence and the use of a geomantic oracle. Malê is quite similar to Malei, yet another line of Quimbanda, reputed to be the most violent and sinister of them all. The chief of this line is Exu Rei and his deputy Exu Marabou. *Marabó* is a term designating a sorcerer amongst Muslims in Sierra Leone and Ghana, equivalent to a juju man. Could it be that several of the lines found in Quimbanda today originate from this small group of Muslims from Yorubaland and Dahomey? We should be careful before jumping to conclusions, but viewing the many similarities between cult, ritual and linguistics does suggest a route similar to that which I have proposed.

The lines do not follow a hierarchy etched in stone. These listings of lineages of spirits seem to be more stable for Exus than for Pomba Giras. The variations in the hierarchies in these lineages are caused predominantly by two factors. Each house of Quimbanda works one specific line, though this does not exclude other impulses. This factor opens up variation between houses. A house working in the line of Malei will be somewhat different from a house that works the line of Souls. They will diverge in focus and in seemingly minor details in the workings and constructions of the spirit-pots. This line-specific work gives a certain flavour to the house and from this the hierarchy can change in conformity with the line and the spirit which oversees the tronco. This is the second factor that invites variation. To exemplify this, in our house the chief is Exu Mór, but the tronco is Pomba Gira Rainha das Sete Encruzilhadas who works in the line of Malei. With Exu Mór establishing himself as the governor of the house, a dual tronco was established that gave our work a basic affinity with the line of the Cemetery, while my Exu belongs to the line of Mossorubi and my Pomba Gira to the line of Nagô. This means is that even if one was consecrated in one specific line, one's spirits can enter from other lines and create a unique synthesis and a very different hierarchy. Each Tatá and Yayá of the house is subject to a similar richness of influences, thus each house will be a unique manifestation upon the dictate and flux of spirit. It is possible to follow a consecration either from the line of your Tatá or from the line of your Exu or Pomba Gira, and it is also possible to cross them as spirit deems fit. In all instances it is the spirits that dictate the process of consecration or initiation.

Lines, Kingdoms, Hierarchies, Legions and Transmutation

104 The lines and hierarchies are ways of tracing some order through the spiritual maze. The lines and legions of Quimbanda were developed as a reflection of the classical hierarchies and denominations developed in Umbanda. The lines are ways of establishing chains of command, or manifestations, and it is not unthinkable that a vague understanding of the Neoplatonic chain of being was used as a blue print for this order. Roughly the lineages are as follows, as understood by the influential Umbandista Lourenço Braga in 1951:

The First Line
is the line of Saints and Oxala ruled by Jesus Christ. Later Braga also added Apollo as a joint ruler of this lineage. Braga says this line is mainly composed of priests, ecclesiastical clergy and devout Catholics. We find many of these spirits in Quimbanda, he says, due to their work of lessening the harmful ways of the spirits of Quimbanda. We find here seven saints, each of whom oversees a legion. These are St. Anthony of Padua, St. Cosmo and Damian (the twins), St. Rita, St. Catarina, St. Expedito, St. Benedict and St. Francisco of Assisi who also goes by the name Simirômba which might reveal the survival of a Congo influence.

of Iamanjá is ruled by the Holy Virgin, Mother of Christ, and given Diana as its co-ruler. Here the hierarchies are more detailed as each legion is also given an appointed ruler. These spirits take particular care of all people working with water, whether as sailors and fishermen, or making the *amaci* (the herbal baths). It is dominated by female spirits and focuses on the untying of magic done with the aid of water, which are generally emotional conditions and issues of poverty. The seven legions within the line are as follows:

- *Legion of Sirens* which is ruled by the Orixa Oxún, spirit of sweetness and the erotic.
- *Legion of Undines* which is ruled by Orixa Nana Burucu, spirit of healing, mother of Omolu.
- *Legion of Caboclas* (female native Indians) of the Ocean which are ruled by Indaiá. This cabocla is said to manifest in the white feathers of predatory birds, sacred to Oxossi, spirit of the hunt.
- *Legion of Caboclas* of the river is ruled by Iará who is the subject of rich folklore. Due to jealousy of her beauty she was chased away from her city and hid in the Amazonian river where she turned into a siren. Iará is cultivated not only in Umbanda but in the greater scope of encantaria and catimbó, being a siren and a mermaid of the sweet waters.
- *Legion of the Sailors* is ruled by Tarimá. This is a class of shy but unpredictable marine spirits that hide in the sand in the deep places of the ocean floor. Some say they have fangs and are of an unruly temperament.
- *Legion of Calungas* is ruled by Calunginha, *she who owns the oceans*, and this mystery should at this point be emphasised.
- *Legion of the Guiding Star* is ruled by Mary Magdalene. This guiding star is commonly a reference to the star of the Magi Kings, but is also synonymous with the hexagram, or star of David, and also with stella maris. Conjoined it gives this legion a very Venusian character bathed in moonlight.

is the line of the Orient which is ruled by St John the Baptist and here we find a great number of nationalities. Hindu, Egyptian, Aztec, Eskimo, Asian, European, Gaul, Roman and North African are all distributed over the seven legions. The second and seventh legion call for further attention. The second legion consists of scientists and doctors and is ruled by Joseph of Arimathea who is working this rulership under guidance from Rafael, the Archangel. The seventh legion is ruled by the caboclo Itaraiaci and the natives of Caraibas, most likely from the Tupi *kara* which means wise, or cunning. From this line the idea of pagan Exus was developed as it is from this line all occultism is to be found. Braga sees this knowledge as connected with the idea of charity.

106   *The Fourth Line*

is the line of Oxossi and counts seven known indigenous nations in Brazil, such as Guarani and the Tupinambás. It is here we find the native knowledge and also the Caboclo who instructed Zelio in developing Umbanda, Caboclo das Sete Encruzilhadas (Seven Crossroads). Many of the practices of Umbanda, such as passes or cleansings, cures and much of its herbal technology is rooted in this line.

The Fifth Line

of Xangó is under the rulership of St James and St Geronimo and is also given a co-rulership with Zeus/Jupiter. Here we find several caboclos who are reputed to support and execute the law of Quimbanda. We find caboclos in this line to be attributed to natural places of power, such as the wind, waterfalls and sacred stones. These have an avenging character, and are proud spirits concerned with justice, such as Pantera Negra (Black Panther) and various snake spirits.

is of Ogum ruled by St George and given the co-rulership with Mars. It is an interesting line as for many Umbandistas this line is seen as the guardians that gave support to Quimbanda. Depending on which kingdom is worked within it, it is possible to resort to Ogum to support the work and make it stable. We have here Ogum Beira Mar who oversees works at the shores of the ocean, Ogum Rompe Mato who works in the wilderness and woods, Ogum Iará who is found at the rivers, Ogum Megê, Ogum Naruê, Ogum de Malei and Ogum de Nagô – which all oversee works in the various lines of Quimbanda.

is the African line ruled by St Cyprian and here we find the preto velhos and the sorcerous transmission from Africa. They are considered infinitely wise and generous, kind and patient in all things. The legions are as follows:

- *The Legion of the People of the Coast* is ruled by Pai Cabinda.
- *The Legion of the People of Congo* is ruled by Rei de Congo.
- *The Legion of the People of Angola* is ruled by Pai José.
- *The Legion of the People of Bengal* is ruled by Pai Bengal.
- *The Legion of the People from Moçambique* is ruled by Pai Jerônimo.
- *The Legion of the People of Luanda* is ruled by Pai Fransisco.
- *The Legion of the People of Guiné* is ruled by Sun Guiné.

It is from these hierarchies and legions that the hierarchies and legions of Quimbanda took shape. And it is by seeing the rich syncretic powers moving Umbanda that we can understand how the synthesis between the goetic spirits of *Verum* was applied to the Exus. The lines of Quimbanda largely define the male hierarchies whereas Pomba Gira is given the role as the co-ruler side by side with the head of each legion and line. This presentation of the lines of Umbanda is given here as they reflect the inherent dynamic nature of Pomba Gira in a better way that the Quimbanda lines and legions. I feel she is better applied from the perspective of the kingdoms.

A kingdom is a place of power where we find concentrations of these spirits. In Pomba Gira's case we are speaking of spirits of sulfur and enchantments. In spite of sulfur's masculine traits in alchemy, it is the fieriness we are looking for here. Sulfur is what gives quicksilver its colour, in a manner of speaking, and thus manifests or fixates the volatile nature of quicksilver. She is fire that brings forth form. This finds support in the alchemical position that sulfur contains the gold of the spirit in its ungestated form. Only dissolving it in quicksilver liberates it, so that it then becomes active and serves as a ferment. This ferment is what the alchemist called *the poisonous dragon* due to its capacity to devour everything. If we see Pomba Gira as the sulfur to Exu's quicksilver this will reveal to us that she is the spirit of celestial ferment. This embraces concepts such as Eros and the Holy Spirit.

This makes the dove symbolism attributed to her infinitely beautiful. If follows from this line of thought that a more deep presentation of the lines of Quimbanda is better discussed in relation to Exu.

First Line – the Line of Malei, headed by Exu Rei
This line is said to be related to the practices of Catimbó and has lately gained a reputation of being a school of black magic, a dark side of Quimbanda, or the worst of the worst, if you will. This reputation can however be disputed, as the line consists of some of the most wise and benign powers of all the legions. These spirits are associated with reptilian spirits of the night, and also with beast-like developments of men upon death. It is said that some people do not turn into pure souls upon death, but rather become creatures of nightmare. This line is said to consist of the sorcerers and witches of Kimbanda and Kiumbanda. Some say that these spirits are a high council amongst the Exu and they are organised as follows:

1 · *Exu Rei das Sete Encruzilhadas*
2 · *Exu Marabô*
3 · *Exu Mangueira*
4 · *Exu Tranca Ruas das Almas*
5 · *Exu Tiriri*
6 · *Exu Veludo*
7 · *Exu dos Rios or Campinas*
Pomba Gira · *Pomba Gira Rainha das Sete Encruzilhadas*

Second Line – the Line of Souls, headed by Omolu
This line works with the transition of souls between the planes; as such, all of these Exus are *omolus* in the sense of being related to the Cemetery. The work of amalá, ebó and various sacrifices are approached through these Exus. They are also excellent teachers in the art of mediumistic skills. They are organised in the following way:

1 · *Exu Mirim*
2 · *Exu Pimenta*
3 · *Exu Sete Montanhas*
4 · *Exu Ganga*
5 · *Exu Kaminaloá*
6 · *Exu Malê*
7 · *Exu Quirombô*
Pomba Gira · *Pomba Gira das Almas*

Third Line – the Line of the Cemetery, headed by Exu Caveira
These spirits live in the cemetery and take the form of skulls and skeletons. They share many features with Exu Caveira, who is the king of the cemetery. These spirits are organised as follows:

1 · *Exu Tatá Caveira*
2 · *Exu Brasa*
3 · *Exu Pemba*
4 · *Exu do Lodo*
5 · *Exu Carangola*
6 · *Exu Arranca Toco*
7 · *Exu Pagão*
Pomba Gira · *Pomba Gira Rainha dos Cemitérios*

Fourth Line – the Line of Nagô, headed by Exu Gererê
This line is reputed to be one of the more advanced of the lines, being
from the area of Nagô on the border of Benin and Nigeria. These
Exus control the magical arts, astral travel and are well versed in the
art of Vodou. Exu Gererê is often confused with Exu Ganga and these
spirits are said to be Gangas as well, in the meaning of sorcerer or
medicine man. The truth is that this Exu was a Vaudogan of Nagô
origin. The line is said to be very hard, demanding and dangerous and
to be a very African manifestation of these spirits.

1 · *Exu Quebra Galho*
2 · *Exu Sete Cruzes*
3 · *Exu Gira Mundo*
4 · *Exu dos Cemitérios*
5 · *Exu da Capa Preta*
6 · *Exu Curadô*
7 · *Exu Ganga*
Pomba Gira · *Pomba Gira Maria Padilha*

Fifth Line – the Line of Mossorubi, headed by Exu Kaminaloá
This line consists of spirits related to the power of the mind, diseases,
insanity and dreams, and there is much Arabic influence within it.
Spirits of Asia are said to be found amongst them. Whenever you
need to focus your mind or attack another person's mind to cause in-

sanity and delusion, cancer or diseases of the blood, these spirits know the ways. The spirits of this line are as follows:

1 · *Exu dos Ventos*
2 · *Exu Morcego*
3 · *Exu Sete Portas*
4 · *Exu Tranca Tudo*
5 · *Exu Marabá*
6 · *Exu Sete Sombras*
7 · *Exu Calunga*
Pomba Gira · *Pomba Gira Maria Mulambo*

Sixth Line – the Line of Caboclos Quimbandeiros, headed by Exu Pantera Negra

This line consists of Indians and Kimbandeiros, who are experts in the art of healing, cursing and shape shifting. These spirits often take the role of personal guides for the people they choose to walk with. The legends say that most of these spirits were more occupied with harming than healing when they walked upon the earth. These spirits are the following:

1 · *Exu Sete Cachoeiras*
2 · *Exu Tronqueira*
3 · *Exu Sete Poeiras*
4 · *Exu da Matas*
5 · *Exu Sete Pedras*
6 · *Exu do Cheiro*
7 · *Exu Pedra Negra*
Pomba Gira · *Pomba Gira da Figueira*

Seventh Line – the mixed Line, headed by Exu dos Rios or Exu Campinas
This line does not only consist of Exus in the strict sense of the word, but of Kiumbas, enchanted spirits that upon death became servitors of Exu. As such, they are related to malefic spirits or demonic entities of crude composition that can be used in works of attack and malefica. These spirits can also become guides and teachers for the kimbandeiro, but they have a reputation of being unreliable, as they feed upon destruction, obsession and havoc. It is not possible to list the names of spirits of this line as they seek out the kimbandeiro along personal paths and the working between the Tata and the kiumba needs to be restricted to the Tatá and his Exu and Pomba Gira.

Her Queendoms

112   When it comes to Pomba Gira it is common to operate with seven or nine queendoms. There are some variations to be found, but I have arrived at the following sensible division that generates a field large enough for lesser kingdoms to unfold within these nine divisions

The Kingdom of the Cemetery
(Cemiterio/Caveira) is headed by Exu Caveria and Maria Padilha Rainha dos Sete Cruzerios da Calunga also known as Pomba Gira Rainha dos Cemiterios. We find in this kingdom spirits that possess knowledge of death and its powers. It is to these spirits we go when we seek knowledge of this kingdom. They are more akin to the nation of Gedé we find in Vodou, a class of living dead that can serve as sources for healing and for taking the burdens of life from our shoulders. The Pomba Giras we find here, such as Rosa Caveira, all have a story to tell that makes life more bearable and death more comprehensible. It is to this kingdom we go if we seek to heal people, or send them to their grave.

The Kingdom of the Crossroads

(Encruzilhadas) is ruled by Exu das Sete Encruzilhadas and Pomba Gira Rainha das Sete Encruzilhadas. This kingdom is deeply connected to the line of Malei.

The Kingdom of the Sepulchures

(Sepulture/Catacombs/Night/Calunga Pequena) is tied to Exu Marabó and Exu Rei through its connection with Malei and Omolu through the line of souls. This class of spirits is said to possess wings. Pomba Giras with wings always come with a more sinister streak and the spirits are considered to be suspicious and volatile by nature.

The Kingdom of the Lyre

(Figueira/Lira/Inferno) is presided over by Maria Padilha Rainha dos Sete Infernos. The Kingdom of the Lyre is headed by Exu Lucifer, and has an intimate relationship with the 5th line headed by Exu Kaminaloá which is so close that some state these two Exus share dominion over these two kingdoms. It is in this kingdom we find Ze Pelintra (but in the service of the line of souls) due to one of his legends telling how he suffered death in the aftermath of the death of his beloved. We also find in this kingdom the pagan spirits, like Pomba Gira Pagã and Maria Navalha.

The Kingdom of the Streets

(Cigana/Malandros/Streets) Pomba Gira Rainha Cigana presides over this kingdom and here we find the line of Nagô. These spirits are those that gravitate towards humans. It is here we find mature knowledge of being that can expand our understanding of life so we can master ourselves. We find here entertainers and the *moleque* (streetsmart ones/urchins), as much as those with a compassionate inclination towards the state of being human.

The *Kingdom of the Wilderness*
(Mata/Mulambo/Queteria) ruled by Exu das Campinas and das
Matas. We find here Maria Mulambo and a flux from the 6th line
of Caboclos Quimbandeiros. We find here manifestations of Pomba
Gira such as Maria Queteria, Maria Queteria das Sete Facas (of Seven
Knives), Pomba Gira das Matas and Pomba Giras associated with cer-
tain plants. These include herbs like Malva, Belladonna, Sete Sangrias,
Datura, Convolvulus and Digitalis – any plant that is subject to par-
ticular attention from the spirit of sulphur. We also find the Pomba
Gira Ganga in this kingdom.

The *Kingdom of the Soul* (Cru-
zeiro/Alma) is headed by Omolu and Maria Padilha Rainha dos
Almas. We find here a great number of saints, and the Church as a
114   field for sorcery is opened in this kingdom. The African line is vibrant
here, as is the mystery of death as advisor. It is an excellent kingdom
for healing and for spirit communication.

The *Kingdom of the Oceanshore*
(Praia) is ruled by Pomba Gira Rainha da Praia and draws on Exu
Gerere and the line of Nagô. You find here Pomba Giras associated
with the waves and winds playing over the waters, communication and
matters of the heart.

The *Kingdom of the Calunga*
(Ocean) is presided over by Pomba Gira Rainha da Calunga and Exu
Calunga. This kingdom also reveals a connection with bat spirits
and the kingdom of sepulchures. We find here Pomba Giras associated with the tide and with the moon, forgotten knowledge and the
mystery of absence.

All these kingdoms have their respective days where they are considered to be more active and accessible; this also has consequences for the types of spirit congress we search for.

Mondays are considered particularly auspicious for any work with souls, so both Cruzerio and Praia are most accessible on this day.

Tuesdays are given to St Antony and the kingdom of the wilderness. It is a day when Quimbanda is good to use in works of protection and defense.

Wednesdays belong to the City of dust, a term referring to Calunga, but also the kingdom of sepulchures. It is an good day for works of communication and to sow discord and confusion.

Thursdays belong to the kingdom of the streets; by virtue of its Nagô orientation, it is considered an auspicious day for any positive work.

Friday belongs to the Encruzilhadas, and is the day most favoured to work with Pomba Gira especially in works of binding. It is also on this day that the Queen of the Seven Crossroads is in alignment with that infernal principle that supports her, the Queen of the Fig Tree in Hell.

Saturday belongs to the Lyre and to the Ocean. It is a day where one's guiding spirit can be placated by going to the Ocean with nine coins and nine white roses which are given in return for protection and inspiration.

Sundays are particularly sacred to the kingdom of Souls but also invite the more benevolent sides of the Crossroad spirits.

The Stone of Quimbanda Ganga

There is one mystery that should be commented upon here, it is Exu/Pomba Gira Ganga. The Pomba Gira working within this mystery is Ganga Mulambo, a form of Maria Mulambo that is said to be most ruthless. The Ganga mystery is said to be Nagô, but even though ascribed to this line, the mystery is of a Congo origin. The flavour of this mystery is very 'vodouesque' and this spirit comes across as a form of St George/Ogum. This spirit is amazingly stern and solid and borders on obsessive in strategy, defence and attack. I mention this because I have deliberately left out Ogum in this treatise, in favour of this spirit. I have personally had good results using this spirit in place of Ogum and conceive him as filling the shoes of Ogum in Quimbanda. In Umbanda, Ogum is considered to be the gatekeeper of all kingdoms of Exu. It is he who permits the crossroads, and kingdoms, to be active in the fire of Pomba Gira. This can take the shape of a ceremony for Ogum, or one can leave a token of recognition of him upon entering the chosen kingdom. You can also use Exu Ganga as the one who protects the working and your door. You will then draw his ponto on your front door with pemba or chalk, spray it with cachaça and sing his ponto. This will be sufficient to protect the work and induce stability. This mystery is also related to twins and the kingdom of the wilderness. You can make a small representation of him by going to the wilderness in the last hour of the day, pay your way in with tobacco, money and whiskey and search out a black stone. Pay for it and take it home. Anoint the stone with palm oil and peppers while singing his ponto. Place the rock in an alguidar and present two curved swords and two identical dolls, one black and one red. This representation can then be used instead of drawing the ponto on your door. His ponto is also used in protection and attack, both from human beings and hostile spiritual forces, something that might come in handy for some.

Ponto Cantado of Exu Ganga

> *Ganga lelè, Ganga lelè*
> *Ele è Egù Ganga*
> *Ganga lelè, Ganga lelè*
> *Ele è Egù Ganga.*

Ponto Riscado of Exu Ganga

The Pomba Giras in the Catalogue

Catalog Spiritu Pombanzila

THE QUEEN OF THE KINGDOM OF THE LYRE is seen by many
as the most pure and ideal manifestation of Pomba Gira.
This queen is the wife of Exu Seven Lyres and some say Seven
Lilies – better known as Exu Lucifer, brother of Exu Mor, also
known as Nine Luzes (Nine Lights). Interestingly, the lyre can
mean three things: it can be the lyre, it can be the lily and it can
also be the little district Lira close to Baganda in Angola. This
is her crossroad, the lyre being a symbol for her seductiveness and
affinity with dance and the arts. The lily is clearly a reference to her
potency for macumba and lastly, the African district that manifests
the three legs of her preferred crossroad, where three worlds meet
and make nine kingdoms. The greatest crossroad is the one that marks
the transition from life to death and as the voluptuous and wise spirit
at this crossing she is always found at the *campo santo*, the cemetery.

In this section I will provide a catalogue of the most well known
Pomba Giras and some of the most obscure ones. The obscure ones
do not have formal pontos cantados as they use Rainha Maria Padilha
or Rainha das Sete Encruzilhadas as intercessor and we will walk on
these points to seek communication. If they accept, the doors will be

opened and they will teach you the secrets that make part of the inner fire of the cult – whether the fire of the stars, or the fires of hell.

In the spirit catalogue I will give descriptions of many Pomba Giras, and you will also find several workings, baths and herbal remedies to give you a clearer idea of the nature of each of the Pomba Giras. At the core of her preferences we find the colours red black and gold. She is drawn towards sulfur, roses, perfumes, bronze, gold, brass, coins, champagne, anis and sweet intoxicating smells. She is particularly active on Fridays and Mondays, where the latter is a day for money and the former a day for love. This also relates to classical correspondences where Friday is ruled by Venus and love and Monday is ruled by the Moon which represents the principle of monetary increase.

The lists of Pomba Giras are extensive, and we find legion upon legion within the lines and kingdoms. This will be demonstrated using Maria Padilha as an example, as she is a general intercessor for all of the Pomba Giras. I will not present every single one of these spirits, but only present a list of the most famous ones to show the dynamic within her manifestations.

It should also be said that many of these songs can be used for other Pomba Giras, by altering their names. As will be evident there are several songs that send the spirits back that can be applied as one sees fit. I will also, when appropriate, discuss the syncretic attempts at conflating them with demonesses. These syncretisms should be approached as thematic, suggestive and not as direct correspondences. So, welcome to the many kingdoms of the most beautiful Pomba Gira!

· Pomba Gira Maria Padilha ·
Also known as Rainha de Castela

Pomba Gira Maria Padilha is amongst the most famous of all Pomba Giras and is close to the archetypical European witch, such as the witches of Évora and those of the Basque country. Her fame is due to her efficacy in rituals and the swift acccomplishment of desires. Her form is similar to women like the Marquesa de Santos, the mistress of Dom Pedro II, whose story we have previously told.

Umbanda workings have demonstrated that this force flows very elegantly and well if one incorporate Ogum in the workings and asks him to intervene and make the working and its results stable. This is an important observation given that Ogum represents the pure masculine and this energetic circuit is to her liking. There is a mutual respect and delight to be found between these two spirits. Likewise, one can also apply Nkisi Zarabanda in workings with Pomba Gira Padilha. This should give some indication of the constitution needed by the practitioner, or what type of force field is needed to be brought into the sphere of working.

The prototypical Pomba Gira, with her connotation of night and the powers of darkness, finds its reflex in Pomba Gira being the wife of Exu, who was syncretised with the diabolic powers. This is, of course, only a diabolical interpretation of Exu. Noting the fact that African belief systems do not have a devil in the Christian sense, this conception of Exu was clearly influenced by the European obsession with demonology from the 14th to 17th century. This is further displayed in the hierarchy of Quimbanda, where the maioral (supreme chief) is Lucifer and not the Orixa Èsú.

Maria Padilha has her manifestations in every natural kingdom and in all reigns of Quimbanda, and we can therefore find Maria Padilha with the epitaph of *amongst many others*. These are frequently understood as roads, similar to the roads of Orixas in Lucumi.

Maria Padilha Rainha dos 7 Cruzeiros da Calunga (7 Crosses of the Calunga)
· Maria Padilha Rainha das 7 Encruzilhadas (Dona Sete) (7 Crossroads) ·
· Maria Padilha Rainha dos Infernos (Hell) ·
· Maria Padilha Rainha das Almas (Souls) ·
· Maria Padilha Rainha das Portas do Cabaré (the Club) ·
· Maria Padilha Rainha das 7 Navalhas (Seven Razors) ·
· Maria Padilha Rainha da Figueira (Fig Tree) ·
· Maria Padilha Rainha das 7 Catacumbas (Seven Catacombs) ·
· Maria Padilha Rainha dos 7 Liras (Seven Lyres) ·

All Pomba Giras that come down under this name, regardless of their path of manifestation, share a fundamental energy and preferences. The variations are related to specific areas of expertise. For instance, a Pomba Gira of the catacombs will naturally be efficacious in the teaching of necromancy, and Calunga will be more apt to help out in matters of health and trafficking with the dead. A ritual with the intent of appeasing and gaining the favours of a particular energetic expression, that is less able to fulfil one's requests, will work out in unexpected ways. This is an important matter to keep in mind. One should also be aware that the spirits of Quimbanda are sympathetic towards other spirit kingdoms and one can work with Pomba Gira under the supervision of a different deity, such as Omolu who has his domain in the cemetery but is an older and less turbulent force than the Exus and Pomba Giras. This means that the kingdom of Quimbanda consists of spirits that are highly dynamic and amenable to change and well disposed towards alliances. One should never forget that when brought into a personal relationship, they will in many cases temper the worshipper's character by introducing him/her to needed lessons and dilemmas.

In conclusion, these spirits are not evil beings that delight in doing evil, they are amoral in their actions, yet they read the human psyche extremely well and will always work towards the betterment of their adherents.

The spirits of Quimbanda are separated into many kingdoms, and in most cases there is an archetypical Pomba Gira found in every kingdom. The many Marias can be said to form a kingdom in itself, but they also cross over into other kingdoms. For instance Maria Mulambo, Maria Quitéria or Maria Lixeira are all related to strong women that have suffered poverty, but in the end gain supremacy over themselves and status in the spirit world. Maria Mirongueira is a Pomba Gira who works quite uncritically with spells, whilst Maria das Almas is related to the dynamic transgression between life and death. Other Marias, such as Maria da Praia, Maria Cigana, Maria Túnica, Maria Rosa, Maria Colodina, Maria Farrapos, Maria Alagoana, Maria Bahiana, Maria Navalha and many others depending on where in Brazil one is, have in common the image of the strong woman that suffers her way to status.

Also worth mentioning is the transglobal character of Pomba Gira, she is taken from all levels of society and from all colours and cultures. The various Pomba Giras, from base and low levels ascending to the status of a queen, can be found mirrored in her worshippers. In a worshipper with a personal Pomba Gira, for instance Maria Lixeira, the energy should be transformed so that their original energy will in the end be crowned. When the worshipper has gone full circle, from his or her personal Pomba Gira and merged with the royal powers of the queen, they can maintain control over their lower soul and appeal to forces that motivate constructive transformation and change.

Pomba Gira is passionate in helping white women, and often one can see that European women with no connection to Brazil manage to draw these forces quite elegantly into their life. This is perhaps less related to colour than to culture. European women represent the ancestry of Pomba Gira Maria Padilha, so she both easily accesses the one who makes the petition, and with great understanding will aid, help and guide.

Maria Padilha is believed to have gone through a symbolic seven incarnations on earth and many believe that the last one was in the city of Ilheus in Bahia, Brazil where she was murdered by a jealous admirer and found at the door of the local nightclub. Her death was mourned by all but the jealous ones. This belief is related to the œuvre of Jorge Amado and in particular the book *Gabriela, Cloves and*

Cinnamon. In this work we meet the beautiful Gabriela who challenges social norms with her carefree sexual life and resistance to marriage. She commits herself somewhat to Nacib, an older man who adores her. Towards the end of the book Nacib catches her inflagrante with another man but forgives her, as the pain of her absence would be too much to bear. This was in a time when men received judicial pardon without difficulty if they killed an adulterous wife and her lover in a crime of passion. From this perspective, Gabriela releases the woman from the shackles of male tyranny, and beauty and womanhood are victorious. It is from such tales that we can understand her as Queen of the cabaret, of the streets, of Hell, of knives and trickery. In a way she embraces Lucifer's bad reputation to show the truth within by declaring him as her favoured husband. In Pomba Gira there is a reappraisal of what is socially condemned, to elevate it to its true stature. The sequence of incarnations are not confined to Brazil, but are

124 spread out all over the world. Quimbanda developed as a Brazilian cult because Pomba Gira's later incarnations were in Brazil. In light of this we can also understand why these spirits are at times called *catiços* or enchanted ones – and this is perhaps a term better applied to Pomba Gira than Exu.

Any women who is subject to jealousy, adoration, abuse or harassment is somehow touched by Pomba Gira and will gain great benefits from exploring her mystery. It is, however, important to emphasise that Pomba Gira likes love, men, clubbing, money and jewels – because she deserves them. So, one caution must be kept in mind by women when they set out to understand themselves using her as their mirror, and this is related to social conditioning. What you deny for yourself due to conformity to social norms and morals, in other words the social cloak you wear to cover your real aspirations, will provoke her. In such cases she places both abusers and bad men with money in your path. She seeks to turn you into a self-assertive woman who only holds natural reserve, whilst she debunks any socially imposed shame or reservations. A woman imprisoned by her guilt, morality, by society or shame is a project for her. This must be crystal clear when you start to work with her as a mirror for your aspiration. You must be calm enough to mediate between challenge and truth. She embraces social condemnation to reveal a different vista. Are you prepared for that? Are you prepared to challenge the social judgments passed upon woman for decades to find yourself? Accepting these terms you will be forged into a model of freedom for others by allowing your true self to shine. But be aware that she will always bring you to the crossroad where you risk renouncing old lies and taking on new ones. She is the principle of attraction and seduction, and constant contemplation on this should make part of any constructive work with Pomba Gira as a muse.

Roads & Legions

The extension into roads, and their aspects, give rise to legions, but they also overlap. The tendency is that legions are not called Pomba Gira but rather, Maria. This is the most common name in Brazil for girls, and it speaks of the triumph of the common.

In the case of Queen Maria Padilha we find the following legions under her command. These legions seem to be more flexible in the case of Pomba Gira than Exu. At least, my experience is that the Exus have a greater affinity with the hierarchies, while Pomba Giras are not so occupied with such limits. They are more concerned with obedience to the Queens, so it seems that they are following a very traditional approach of respect, based upon age and status in the fold. An example of a legion used in one house of Umbanda/Quimbada is as follows:

> *Maria Molambo*
> *Maria Quitéria*
> *Maria Lixeira*
> *Maria Mirongueira*
> *Maria das Almas*
> *Maria da Praia*
> *Maria Cigana*

Maria Tunica
Maria Rosa
Maria Colodina
Maria Farrapos
Maria Alagoana
Maria Bahiana
Maria Navalha

The legions are nuances of the roads, which is why for many of these you make an appeal to Maria Padilha and actually call upon her to release the requested aid. In Umbanda she is constantly spoken of in relation to Ogum, the knight and divine blacksmith, because Ogum represents the idealised strength of the male. He is the rock solid power for protection and honour of the 'Virgin'.

126   There is also another element that should be mentioned in this telling of Maria Padilha. This is the prophecy she gave simultane- ously in several terreiros of Umbanda in Brazil in the first part of the year 2000. There was a wicked consistency in the message that told that she had sentenced 7000 souls to hell and another 7000 to heaven; her work was done and it was time to get rid of the chains of Orixas. She revealed that her true mission was to *convert mankind to its original soul*. She said that her mission was done in white at the feet of Jesus who would bring the souls to the realisation that Lucifer brought light from darkness. She further stated that she will work only in the service of love from now on. I find this prophecy to be quite intrigu- ing as it suggests the return of a pure Quimbanda which destroys the supposed enmity between Jesus Christ and Lucifer. It is a Bogomil redemption found in this prophecy that fortifies the message in this book, that is, of a Quimbanda that strives towards the elevation of the soul.

Pontos Cantados for Maria Padilha

Ela é Maria Padilha,	She is Maria Padilha,
Da sandalinha de pau,	Who wears sandals of wood,
Ela trabalha pro bem,	She works for what is good,
Mais ela trabalha pro mal,	but she works for bad,
Oia Pombagiré, oia pombagiré,	Oia Pombagirá, oia pombagirá,

.

Com uma rosa e um cigarrilho,	With a rose and a cigarette,
Maria Padilha já chegou,	Maria Padilha arrives,
E na Kalunga...	In the Kalunga...
Ela é Rainha...	She is the Queen...
Ela trabalha com muito amor,	She works with much love,
Sete Cruzeiros da Kalunga,	Seven Crosses in the Kalunga,
é a morada dessa Mulher,	is the dwelling of this woman,
Ela é!!!...	She is!!!...
Maria Padilha,	Maria Padilha,
Rainha do Candomblé!!	Queen of Candomblé!!

127

.

Ela é...	She is...
Exu Maria Padilha	Exu Maria Padilha
Exu...	Exu...
E a sua Faca brilha!	And her knife shines!

.

De onde é que a Maria Padilha vem,   Where did Maria Padilha come from,
Aonde é que Maria Padilha mora (×2)   Where is the place Maria Padilha lives,
Ela mora na mina de ouro,   She lives in the mine of gold,
Onde o galo preto canta,   Where the Black cock sings,
Onde criança não chora. (×2)   Where children never cry. (×2)

•

Exu Maria Padilha,   Exu Maria Padilha,
Trabalha na Encruzilhada, (×2)   Works at the Crossroad, (×2)
Toma conta, presta conta...   Takes care, is attentive...
No romper da madrugada,   In the cracks at the end of night,
Pomba Gira minha Comadre,   Pomba Gira my ally,
Firma Fé de noite e dia,   Steady in faith night and day,
É por isso que nós somos,   It is because of this we are,
Da sua feitiçaria   Your sorcery

•

O povo dos Infernos é quem vai levar,   The people of Hell are those who take it,
Levar o que não presta pro Além Mar (×2)   Takes what is not got across the ocean (×2)
Exu Rei da Lira é Lucifer!   Exu King of the Lyre is Lucifer!
Maria Padilha...   Maria Padilha...
Rainha Exu Mulher!! (×2)   Queen Exu Woman!! (×2)

•

Maria Padilha é...	*Maria Padilha is...*
Rainha do Candomblé!	*Queen of Candomblé!*
Maria Padilha mora,	*Maria Padilha lives,*
Nas portas de um Cabaré!	*At the door of the Cabaret!*

.

Maria, Maria Padilha Ela é...	*Maria, Maria Padilha, She is...*
Uma Mulher faceira,	*A Woman coquette,*
Que trabalha Meia Noite e também,	*Who works the midnight as well,*
A madrugada inteira,	*As the whole night through,*
Sete rosas encarnadas,	*Seven flowering roses,*
Vou levar prá essa Maria,	*Will you bring to this Maria,*
Para afastar de mim,	*To tié to me,*
Toda feitiçaria,	*All spell crafts,*
Maria, Maria Padilha Ela é...	*Maria, Maria Padilha She is...*
Caminhou por toda a Terra,	*Wandering all across the world,*
Na Kalunga ela ficou,	*In the Kalunga she stays,*
Lá na Encruza ou lá na Rua,	*There at the cross or in the street,*
Ela é...	*She is found...*
Camarada sua,	*Your alley she is,*
Maria, Maria Padilha Ela é...	*Maria, Maria Padilha, She is...*

129

.

Quem não me respeitar,	*Those who don't respect me*
Oh! logo se afunda,	*Oh, will soon enough sink,*
Eu sou Maria Padilha,	*I am Maria Padilha,*
dos 7 Cruzeiros da Kalunga.	*From the Seven Crosses of the Kalunga.*

Quem não gosta da Maria Padilha...	Who doesn't like Maria Padilha...
Tem, tem que se arrebentar,	She has, has what breaks it all,
Ela é formosa, ela é faceira,	She is beautiful and coquettish,
Oh bela! vem trabalhar.	Oh beautiful! come and work.

·

Moço, você conhece aquela moça,	Boy, do you know that girl,
Que trabalha no escuro,	Who works in the dark,
Olhando osso,	Watching the bones,
Osso por osso,	Bone by bone,
Dente por dente,	Tooth by tooth,
Dia trás dia,	Day after day,
Hora trás hora...	Hour after hour...
Ela é Maria Padilha...	She is Maria Padilha...
Ela é Maria Mulher,	She is Maria the Woman,
Ela trabalha na Figueira,	She works at the Fig tree,
Por ordem de Lucifer.	By the command of Lucifer.

·

Maria Padilha já chegou,	Maria Padilha has arrived,
Trago para Ela uma linda flor,	Bring to her the most beautiful flower,
Festa no Terreiro, festa no gongá,	The party is in the Terreiro, party in the gongá,
Chegou Maria Padilha para todo mal levá.	When Maria Padilha arrives she takes away evil.

·

Maria Padilha caminhou...	*Maria Padilha walked...*
7 vezes	*7 times*
Maria Padilha trabalhou...	*Maria Padilha worked...*
7 vezes	*7 times*
Maria Padilha assobiou...	*Maria Padilha whistled...*
7 vezes	*7 times*
Caminhou, trabalhou, assobiou	*Walked, worked, whistled*
7 vezes (×2)	*7 times* (×2)

Ponto Riscado for manifesting the powers of Maria Padilha

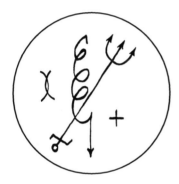

Ponto Riscado to be used when honoring the spirit
and when preparing despacho

Ponto Riscado to use in order to strengthen her presence
and give added stability to the medium

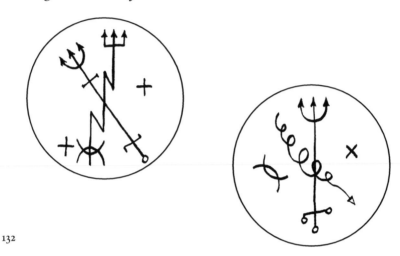

Ponto Riscado of Maria Padilha who triumphs,
used in workings of defence and attack

A Working with Maria Padilha to open one's roads and opportunities

You will need the following:
A black pigeon
A red and black cloth marked with her ponto
Seven extra long cigarettes or cigarillos
Nine red candles
Good quality black, white and red silk cords
A virgin cup
A bottle of anisette
A bottle of cachaça
Seven coins
Tobacco
Seven boxes of matches

This working is better done on a Monday, and invites the attention of the line of souls. You will prepare for this either at the great hour or at dusk. Before the working you will tie up the pigeon with the cords, constantly visualising your own tied-up situation, or the one you are doing the work on behalf of. At the appointed time take all this to the chosen crossroad and give first three coins to the guardians of the crossroad at your right and then three coins to the Queen of the Crossroad. Leave a candle on each side and sprinkle the coins generously with the cachaça. Then lay out your cloth and make a multiple crossing with the silk cords. Arrange the candles around it and place the cup in the middle. Organise the matches around the cup in such a way that the heads of seven matches are left visible. Then take the anisette and fill the cup until if splashes over the cloth and place the bottle at its side. Light the candles and the cigarettes. You will now sing to her and bring the pigeon to her attention. Untie it while explaining the situation, ask her to open the ways for whomever the pigeon represents. When the pigeon is untied, bless it and sacrifice it to Maria Padilha as you promise a better present when the roads are clear. Rise up, take three steps backwards, turn around and leave the crossroad. Take a bath in basil and coconut water upon coming home, and allow a white candle to burn at the side of your bed throughout the night.

Every natural kingdom has a King and a Queen. Experience indicates
that the Pomba Gira Queens are the most respected of the Exus and
Pomba Giras, and even the majority of Exus bow down humbly to
them. The queens are demanding, and generous, they work fast and to
the point. The usual format for working with the queens is to present
small gifts in the working and make promises of what you will bring
to her after the request has been accomplished. Offerings are usually
made in multiples of seven (sometimes nine or three) and one is usually advised to place them at the seventh crossroad from one's house,
terreiro or place of working, so they can automatically go to the feet
of Pomba Gira Sete Encruzilhada

When you make a working of Quimbanda, the point of your working becomes charged with this energy as the centre point. The sacred
space is defined outward from this point. In the case of our house of
Quimbanda, it is situated exactly at a split in the road, exactly in a gate
under the slope of a hill. In the surrounding area there is a river, a
wood, a T-crossroad, a swamp and a lake. From the point of worship
all these natural sites turn into resting places for Exu and Pomba Gira
as Venus rises and night falls, preferably on Fridays and Mondays in
the case of Pomba Gira. These are days when the land is changing and
planetary benevolence is more readily at hand.

Failing to accommodate the promises made to Pomba Gira can
in the worst cases be fatal, but usually culminates in situations that
are highly annoying and troublesome, as havoc enters your life. The
higher in rank the spirit, the more havoc and disturbance will be
unleashed.

134

Pontos Cantados for Pomba Gira Rainha

Meu sinho, meu sinhozinho,   My bell, my little bell,
Gargalharam na encruzilhada,   Laughing at the crossroad,
Gargalharam na encruzilhada,   Laughing at the crossroad,
Era Pomba Gira Rainha, sinhô,   She is Pomba Gira Queen, the bell,
Que reinava na madrugada (×2)   Who rules the darkest hours of night

    ·

Aué, Pomba Gira Rainha,   Aué Pomba Gira Queen,
Comanda a madrugada,   Who commands the night,
Comanda a madrugada,   Who commands the night,
Quando nas encruzas,   When the crossings are made,
Dá logo a sua gargalhada.   Your laughter is not far away.

    ·

Queiram bem a Exu,   Good wishes from Exu,
Queiram bem a Exu, gente,   Good wishes from Exu, people,
Queiram bem a Exu, gente,   Good wishes from Exu, people,
Eu quero Dona Rainha,   I want the Lady Queen,
Queiram bem a Exu, gente.   Good wishes from Exu, people.

Ponto Riscado for manifesting her powers

Ponto Riscado that can be used in works
of attraction and magnetism

Ponto Riscado used when one needs to
break up difficult situations or people

The Pomba Gira of the Seven Crossroads is a Queen whose name is truly legion. The importance of the crossroad and the number seven is here merged, and she is an ultimate Queen, the sum of all aspiration for the adherents of Pomba Gira. She is a strong, harsh, generous, wise and murderous queen that takes delight in demonstrating the power of womanhood in front of men, especially those who focus their attention on their genitals. This Pomba Gira is the kind of woman that gladly displays her firm breasts and opens her legs to any man, only to deliver a deadly blow to his neck if he approaches her in ways unsuited to her majesty. She is ruled by a sense of justice and vengeance. The Pomba Giras of the Seven Crossroads are amazingly powerful. They can be employed to do almost any kind of work and they are deeply related to destiny – the crossroads being synonymous with the crossroads we face in life. More than anything, she helps people find a way out of miserable situations, and guides the steps that lead to a fulfilling life. She can be used in the red rites (love and potions, bindings and separations) as well as in situations where things are crossed and one can see few solutions. She is also helpful in court-cases. She can be the best of friends and the worst of enemies.

137

Pontos Cantados for Pomba Gira Rainha das Sete Encruzilhadas

Eu sou Rainha	*I am the Queen*
Nos Sete Encruzos	*of Seven Crossings*
Em cada um	*And each one*
Tenho uma morada	*Has a dweller*
Eu quero filho para defender	*I want children to defend*
E inimigo para espetar	*And enemies to impale*
Eu é a Rainha das 7 Encruzilhadas	*I am the Queen of Seven Crossroads*
É lá que eu faço minha morada	*It is there I make my dwellers*

Ò gira formosa	*Oh the beautiful movements*
Tem alegria e rosa	*Hath joy and roses*
Na gira de Pomba Gira	*In the celebration of Pomba Gira*
Você vem balançar	*You will come to shake*
No balanço de Pomba Gira	*In the shaking of Pomba Gira*
Sua chamada vai rolar, vai rolar	*Her call will roll and roll again*

.

Meu caminho e de fogo	*My path is of fire*
No meio da Encruzilhada	*In the middle of the crossroad*
Quem quiser me demandar	*Who wants to command me*
Cuspo e vou ihe pisar	*Spit and I Will step on you*
Quanto inimigo na Terra	*How many enemies on earth*
Querendo desafiar	*Wanting to challenge*
Sou pomba Gira formosa	*This beautiful Pomba Gira*
Formosa para Ihe quebrar	*Beautiful enough to break you*

138

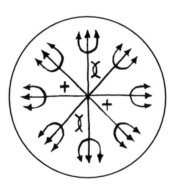

Ponto Riscado of Pomba Gira Rainha das Sete Encruzilhadas
to be used when her powers are needed

Ponto Riscado of Pomba Gira Rainha das Sete Encruzilhadas
to be used during appeal and worship

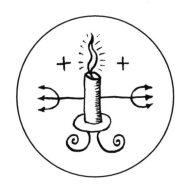

Ponto Riscado of Pomba Gira Rainha das Sete Encruzilhadas
used when workings are done with her in the cemetery

A working to get rid of bothersome people

You will need the following:
One white candle
A dozen red candles
A dozen black candles
Cigars
Tostão
A bottle of anisette or red wine
Seven cigarillos
A black cloth
8 boxes of matches
7 roses, open and free of thorns
I white pemba
I virgin chalice

Bring the above with you to the cemetery at dusk or midnight on a Friday. Prior to leaving you need to light a white candle in your house in honour of your spirit guides. Place a glass of water and one of cachaça by the candle and pray for support in the work you will undertake.

At the gate of the cemetery ask licence of the guardian of the gate and leave him a candle and three tostão. Drop the coins one by one and stamp the ground with your left foot with the fall of each coin. Then light one red and one black candle and offer a lit cigar. You have now bought your entrance to the campo santo/calunga and so now you remove your shoes. You then go to the Cruzeiro and here offer candle and cigar, asking that the kiumbas be released to aid in your demand. You then go to the back of the Cruzeiro and salute Omolu and offer candle and cigar asking for protection and steadiness in your working. At the left side of the Cruzeiro you will spread out the cloth

and write the name of the bothersome person crossed over itself seven times. Arrange seven black and seven red candles around it. Call Rainha Sete Encruzilhadas and light the candles. Place the boxes of matches by the candles, and one in the centre together with the chalice. Light the cigarillos and place by the side of the candles. Take the roses and place one by each candle and place the anisette on top of the name.

Sing to her and present your request, slowly pouring the anisette into the chalice until the bottle is empty. This being done you thank the attending spirits and leave, taking seven steps backward. Turn around, put your shoes back on and leave the cemetery. Greet the guardian of the gate as you leave. Upon returning home, do not enter without having had the kiumbas and ghost attached to you during this work removed by having holy water thrown to your left, right and over your head, followed by the same procedure with sea salt. Then take a bath in salt water mixed with petals of white roses and basil.

This kind of work can easily bring negativity to your household, and you may notice this either in an increase in obsession with the bothersome person, or an increase in anger. Embark on a daily regime of spiritual baths for as long as needed, whether three or seven days. During this time the unwanted presence will start to fade from your life. This working can also be done with Pomba Gira Calunga, Calunga Pequena and Cruzeiro.

Pomba Gira of the Encruzilhada is a highly effective entity with a great power to create movement. We might perceive her as a more serpentine and softly sliding influence than the Queen of Seven Crossroads. She is found in various manifestations in different kingdoms, which subtly alters her temperament. Hence, this Pomba Gira is found at the oceanshore (Praia), at the Cemetery (Calunga), and also as Maria Mulambo de Encruzilhada and countless others. She is found in all intersections where two or more roads form a cross, either in a T or an X junction. She is not one, she is legion. She is a trusted companion and helps her devotees to find structure and a right course in life. She can interfere in legal issues and find cures to difficult issues, dissolve debts and turn her devotee into a victorious opponent. She is said to be one of the red witches, working within the streams of malefica and love magic, both in separation and bindings.

Friday is her day of honour and her offerings are placed at crossroads. One should also keep in mind that the magical power of this Pomba Gira is of an extreme nature as she both easily possesses limbs and also enjoys working on the more esoteric levels within the consciousness of the devotee.

Pontos Cantados for Pomba Gira Da Encruzilhada

Na encruza eu vou chegar,	*At the crossing I will come,*
Com meu garfo vou espetar,	*With my trident I will impale,*
Ao inimigo vou demandar,	*The enemy you appoint,*
Arrastando-o pelas ruas,	*Dragging it in the streets,*
Deixando-o estraçalhar.	*Tearing it to pieces.*
Eu me chamo Pomba Gira da Encruzilhada,	*I am known as Pomba Gira of the Crossroad*
Na Quimbanda vou trabalhar,	*In Quimbanda I Will work,*
E todo trabalho vou desmanchar. (×2)	*And all spells I will untie.* (×2)

Pomba Gira, oh Pomba Gira,	*Pomba Gira, oh, Pomba Gira,*
De onde tu vens? (×2)	*To where will you go?* (×2)
Eu venho lá da encruza,	*I will go to the crossing,*
E sou mulher de Lucifer. (×2)	*I am the wife of Lucifer.* (×2)

•

Eu me chamo Pomba Gira,	*I am called Pomba Gira,*
Da encruzilhada eu sou,	*I am from the Crossroad,*
E na minha encruzilhada,	*It is at my Crossroad,*
Onde tenho minha morada,	*Where I have my dwelling,*
Eu sei trabalhar,	*And know how to work,*
Quebro qualquer demanda	*And break any spell you wish.* (× 2)
se precisar. (× 2)	

Ponto Riscado of Pomba Gira da Encruzilhada used in order to retrieve her power and when doing workings with this entity

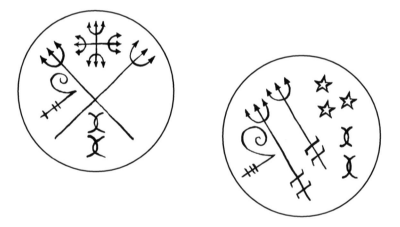

Ponto Riscado to be used when workingwith Pomba Gira da Encruzilhada

Working for undoing a work made to separate two people

Variations of this spell are found in many terreiros and houses of
Quimbanda. Pomba Gira of the Encruzilhada has the power to break
a couple or make a couple, and can also break spells of this kind. This
Pomba Gira is a true expert of the Art and her efficacy is bound to
impress the worshipper. The spell reproduced here is interesting due
to its root working elements.

You will do this spell on a Friday as the hour approaches midnight.
This spell is reported to work well in any lunar phase and you will
need the following items:

300 grams of Popcorn
7 black candles
7 red ribbons
7 cigars
Fresh water (not tap water)
Flour of manioc
Matches
Pomba Gira oil
Black Pemba
Congo powder*
Untie All powder or Abre Caminho
Efun powder/white pemba
A red cloth
A plate with two big coconuts
One bottle of cachaça

Prepare the popcorn and a padé with the flour and the three powders
as well as the water. Then put the padé on a plate and spread with the
popcorn. Set it down in the area where you will do the working and
knock three times on the ground asking that the spirits of the place to

---

* This powder follows a secret formula and is also called Exu Rei powder. This can be
substituted by drying leaves of pennyroyal, fennel, peppers and guiné and crush together. This will approximate the intended vibration.

be favourable to your presence and work. Some will ask permission to Ogum Megé, as in many terreiros that pertain to both Umbanda and Quimbanda, Ogum is seen as the ever loyal guardian of Exu.

Spread the cloth on the earth, mark the four points with the Pomba Gira oil and then trace the ponto on the cloth with the black pemba. Then call on Pomba Gira saying words to the effect of: *Come Pomba Gira of the Encruzilhada, come to dismantle this spell that has been made. You are coming to set free N. Saravá!* You will then clap your hands in a battery of two and seven three times (II IIIIIII × 3). Annoint the candles with the Pomba Gira oil and arrange them around the plate in a triangular form. When lighting the candles sing: *It is me N that is calling Pomba Gira,* seven times. Open the cachaça and pour it in a circle around the offering (the empty bottle will be removed and placed in the garbage). Take seven steps backward and without looking over your shoulder, you will turn around and leave the place.

144   This ritual can be worked once a month for seven months in order to obtain maximum results. This is something to keep in mind both in works of attack as well as when dismantling workings. It takes time. Fast working deities will be able to execute the desired end in about three workings, others over the course of seven workings, and some take more time than this. The point is to saturate the victim over and over again with a constant flow of energies.

It is important to observe that if you do the work explained here, you should not do any other workings for the next seven days, neither say ill of any other person nor harm anyone in any way. If one finds peace of mind to be difficult for this period one is advised to light a white candle and give a glass of water to one's guardian angel every night for seven days praying that the good angel decends into this flame and water and illuminates and protect you. On the seventh day you will take what is left of the candles and dispose of them under a plant.

This Pomba Gira has been related to Pititis in a modern attempt at syncretism. This syncretism is perhaps more proper than many others, as this spirit is a matron of witches in Mexican folklore linking her with another famous figure of magical worship in Mexico and some areas of Latin America, Our Lady of Guadeloupe. The Queen of the Seven Crosses is found in the cemetery and is a rather cold and distant spirit that can manifest in extremely hot and agitated ways. Her stern posture is contrasted by the more gentle ways of the Queen of the Calunga. She lives at the central cross of the boneyard. She works healing very well, but she is a master of the black rites and is well disposed to inflict turbulence in a person's life without them noticing that there is a swarm of malice hovering over their shoulder. She takes good care of her votaries and is an excellent teacher who gives freely from her vaults of wisdom. This Pomba Gira works well under the supervision of Ogum or Omolu. She needs to be contacted in the cemetery and one needs to offer marafo and three coins at the entrance of the cemetery, either to Ogum Megé or to Omolu, in order to be granted access to walk through the kingdom of death and approach the Queen of the Seven Crosses. We use the intervention of Maria Padilha or Sete Encruzilhada in working with her, as she is closely related to these Pomba Giras.

Pontos Cantados for Pomba Gira dos Sete Cruzeiros

Quando eu nasci, eu era formosa,	*When I was born I was beautiful,*
E fui muito sacrificada,	*And was greatly sacrificed,*
Hoje moro no cruzeiro,	*Today I live at the Cross,*
Ao lado de meu Pai Omolu,	*At the side of my father Omolu,*
Ele é Pai e feiticeiro,	*He is father of sorcerers,*
Feiticeiro de muita força e luz,	*Sorcerer of much Power and light,*

Ele é dono de Cruzeiro,	*He is the owner of the Cross,*
Ordenança de Ogum,	*Ordained by Ogum,*
No seu Reino eu vou vivendo,	*In his kingdom I live,*
São as almas que me conduzem,	*And conduct the many souls,*
Eu me chamo Pomba Gira,	*I am known as Pomba Gira,*
Dos Sete Cruzeiros da Calunga.	*Of the seven crosses in the Calunga.*

·

Ela mora no Cruzeiro das Almas,	*She lives at the Cross of souls,*
Ela guerreia sem querer parar,	*She is a warrior unlike any other,*
Tem a força dos Pretos Velhos,	*She has the strength of the ol' blacks,*
E no Cruzeiro ela quer ficar,	*And at the Cross she wants to stay,*
Na morada de Omolu,	*Living with Omolu,*
Omolu, meu Pai Atotô.	*Omolu, my father Atotó.*

·

Eu sou Pomba Gira dos Sete Cruzeiros,	*I am Pomba Gira of the Seven Crosses,*
Da Calunga, minha falange é muito boa,	*From the Calunga my legions are very good,*
Tenho até muitas crianças,	*I even have many children,*
Como Exu, o que venero.	*With Exu, whom I venerate.*

Ponto Riscado for Pomba Gira dos Sete Cruzeiros

A Working to protect the body of your beloved against untimely death

This work is done on a Friday in the cemetery in order to protect people with dangerous occupations or who are involved in risky activities. The ritual needs to be done once a month for three consecutive months, observing day and lunar phase. You will need to prepare popcorn mixed with dendê and cornflour, approximately equal quantities. Bring this with you to the cemetery. Ask license to Ogum Megê or Exu Porteira before you enter with 24 red roses (no thorns), seven red candles, seven red ribbons, one white candle, a baton, cigars, and a few bracelets. Place the red cloth at the side of a grave that attracts you; the grave should be close to the Cruzeiro and have a cross upon it. Set down the plate of popcorn and put all the roses on it, as well as the ribbons. The ribbons should be placed halfway on and halfway off the plate. Light the candles around the ebo and sing her ponto. Light the cigars and place around the ebo and pray for protection. Finally take the baton and say: *May NN not suffer death, therefore I give you the tool of your father Omolu so you can defend NN from death's blow.* Take a bottle of cachaça and pour it on the ground as a thanksgiving to Omolu. Leave the working place and repeat three times on a monthly basis.

This name means Queen of the Little Water or Queen of the Little Cemetery. In Quimbanda the word *calunga* is usually translated as cemetery, whilst keeping in mind the ancestral ocean.

This Pomba Gira has been associated with Lilith, one of the less sensible syncretisms, the fusion between them is perhaps brought about by an identification of shared erotic connections between Lilith and this Pomba Gira.

Calunga Pequeña has her kingdom at the bottom of the ocean, where the spirits of those that died at sea are under her domain. She is said to appear in the form of a mermaid or a talking sea creature, and is accordingly related more to the native Indian myths of amphibian shapeshifters and the sirens of Greek legend who lured sailors to their deaths with seductive song. One can even go so far as considering the movie *Dagon* by Fernández and Yuzna (2000) which in its depiction of the princess of Dunwich gives an interesting and fairly accurate description of this Pomba Gira. She can be worked together with Yemoja or Olokun in order to fortify her workings. She is said to be the queen of a whole tribe of Exus and Pomba Giras that live in kingdoms at the bottom of the ocean and manifest in dangerous, poisonous and unusual sea creatures, for instance monkfish, electric eel, puffer fish and sharks. She rules deep emotions and passions and can work in ways to cause a lost lover to return or a wayfaring husband to come home, with passion and eyes only for you. She can also be used in order to awaken the erotic and sensual urges in a man who has lost interest in you, as well as ignite a new passion in the woman and reawaken desire.

A working with this Pomba Gira should be done at the oceanshore, preferably at a cliff where the water is deep. A place like the cliffs at Buzios in Rio Grande de Norte is an excellent place where the power of this Pomba Gira is very strong. In a place like this you can make a working in order to rekindle the flame of passion in your object of desire by the following ritual, which is found in several sources, both written and oral.

Pontos Cantados for Pomba Gira Da Calunga

Ancorou, ancorou na Calunga,	Set anchor in the Calunga,
Pomba Gira Calunguinha do Mar,	Pomba Gira little Calunga of the Ocean,
Ò, ò, ò, Pomba Gira Calunguinha do Mar,	Ò, ò, ò, Pomba Gira Calunguinha of the Ocean,
Saravá, ò saravá,	Saravá, ò saravá,
Pomba Gira Calunguinha do Mar,	Pomba Gira Calunguinha of the Ocean,
Pomba Gira Calunguinha do Mar,	Pomba Gira Calunguinha of the Ocean.

•

Sa Calunguinha do Mar está na gira,	The graveyard of the Ocean is at the celebration,
Aqui na banda ela chegou,	Here at the point of Power she came,
Trouxe Exu na gira,	Brought Exu to the celebration,
Foi ele mesmo que mandô,	It was indeed He Who sent her,
Foi ele mesmo que mandô.	It was indeed He Who sent her.

•

Quando bater meia noite,	When midnight strikes,
Nesta praia Pomba Gira vai chegar,	On this shore Pomba Gira will come,
Vem buscar os seus presentes,	To search for her gifts,
Vem chegar para demandar,	She is coming to request/to do a working,
Vem Pomba Gira Calunguinha do Mar,	Come Pomba Gira Calunginha of the Ocean,
Vem Pomba Gira Calunguinha do Mar.	Come Pomba Gira Calunginha of the Ocean.

Ponto Riscado to be used when one desires to bring down her powers

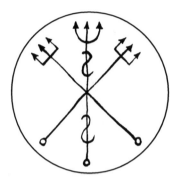

Ponto Riscado for bringing down Pomba Gira da Calunga Mar
to be used in works of unification and prosperity

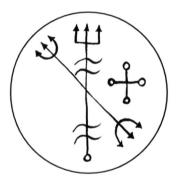

Ponto Riscado for honouring Pomba Gira da Calunga
A Working in order to awaken passion in someone

You will need the following materials:
One red pemba
Three boxes of matches
12 red roses (or white)
Lime
Pomba Gira's Blood oil
Love powder
Passion powder
Mater Dolorosa powder (or Erzulie Freda powder/oil)
Seven red and white candles
One pack of cigarettes
One bottle of cachaça
One bottle of muscatel wine
Two glasses
A terracotta plate

The ritual should be done at the Great Hour preferably on a Monday or a Saturday and using the license of either Yemoja or Ogum Beira Mar, the owner of the ocean itself. When you approach the ocean you will simply light a candle for them, one blue and one red. Stamp the ground or strike it with your hand three times, and ask permission from either of them to enter their kingdom. State your purpose, the name of the spirit you seek to work with, and ask that they walk with you and see that your desires are executed. Then go to an undisturbed place and arrange the ritual. Draw the ponto on the terracotta plate while softly chanting her name. Place three roses on the ponto and focus on your desire, telling her: *Pomba Gira da Calunga, see me, watch me, hear me, as I am here embraced by your power, and inspire in NN passion and desire deep as your power.* Throw the three roses into the water, take the rest of the roses and the cachaça and walk backwards nine steps. Then pour some cachaça on the 9th step and walk towards the place of offering again, pouring some drops of cachaça with each step. Say with each step: *one step closer to arouse the passion in NN*, with the 9th step say: *the last step is done and the passion of fire begun.* Anoint the candles with Pomba Gira oil and light them while singing to her. Place the nine roses on the plate together with the muscatel wine, pouring it over them. Pour the other powders over the roses as well and smear some of it on yourself. Take 12 cigarettes and light them around her offering, and smoke one yourself. In the centre of the offering present the lime and ask her to infuse it with the power of passion and seduction. Pour wine in the two glasses and present one in the centre of the roses and drink the other. While doing this, sprinkle cachaça around the roses and let the bottle stand open amidst them. When the ritual is finished, take the cachaça and lime with you, and with this prepare a caipirinha with sugar for the object of your desire. If the object of desire does not drink, use the lime to make a juice and add three drops of cachaça. This ritual should be performed three times before the full effect is experienced. It is good if you can wash off the scent and such in the ocean on the way back from the ritual under the supervision of Yemoja or Ogum, and make a final prayer to Pomba Gira in the Ocean.

This Pomba Gira is syncretised with Proserpina, who was abducted
by Hades. This would indicate that this Pomba Gira is quite ancient
and is, in her dual observance, a mighty source of wisdom. She knows
both the healing spirits of wood and water, as well as the kingdom of
Omolu, placing this Pomba Gira in a unique position when workings of healing deadly diseases are sought. The Queen of the fields
is deeply related to the fair folk of the land and is, as such, both
kind and dangerous. She should be approached showing respect for
her domain. Her colours are green and dark blue with spots of red.
She works closely with Jurema and Iara and can also be approached
through other caboclos and enchanted ones. It is common to use the
intervention of Exu das Matas when working with her and use the
songs for Pomba Gira Rainha together with proper offerings.

153

Ponto Cantado for Exu/Pomba Gira das Matas

Exu das Matas é,	*Exu of the Wilderness is,*
Exu das Matas é,	*Exu of the Wilderness is,*
Exu das Matas é meu senhor,	*Exu of the Wilderness is my lord,*
Exu das Matas é,	*Exu of the wilderness is,*
Eu vi um clarão nas matas,	*I saw in a clearing in the woods,*
E pensava que era dia, (×2)	*Thinking that it was on this day, (×2)*
Era o Exu das Matas que fazia sua magia. (×2)	*Exu of the wilderness was making his magic. (×2)*

Ponto Riscado for Exu/Pomba Gira das Matas

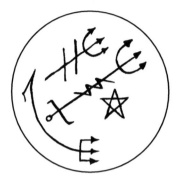

This ponto can be used together with the pontos of Maria Padilha

*Some useful spiritual baths made under the auspicies of Maria Padilha
and Exu and Pomba Gira das Matas*

The classic bath for opening opportunities and enabling spirit to
solidify better in one's body during a working can be done by taking
three bottles of cachaça to the crossroad, one black candle and one red
together with three cigars, one white pemba and a black cloth. Ask
licence from the people of the wilderness and the crossroad while
drawing the pontos on the cloth. Place all the offerings on the cloth
and sing to das Matas. Light a cigar and puff some smoke to the heav-
en, then to the four corners and over the cloth and gifts. As midnight
approaches, light the candles and one more cigar and stand naked on
the cloth while you pour the cachaça over your body from the neck
down. Sing and pray and state when you are done that whatever negativity, whatever is hindering your success, will remain here. Allow
yourself to dry in the air and put your clothes back on. Leave the place
and do not return for the remainder of the year to this location.

Salt water is another useful bath for expelling negativity. It can be prepared with water and salt at home or naturally in the ocean itself.

Basil, coconut water and rue make for a most potent infusion that repels negativity and restores tranquillity and clarity of mind.

Likewise a bath of macerated petals of white roses is good, even for small children who suffer from nightmares and spiritual pain.

· *Pomba Gira Rainha da Praia* ·

In the case of this Pomba Gira another meaningless syncretism is made by ascribing Klepoth to her. This Pomba Gira is actually quite calm and far less eruptive than many of her sisters. She is related to Venus born from the foam of waters, and is a highly benevolent spirit closely related to the energetic current of Yemoja. In the stories of this Pomba Gira one can also detect the influence of Greek myth, as she is often given the same attributes as Circe. This Pomba Gira is rich in wisdom and utterly fascinating. She is a harmonious spirit and reluctant to resolve matters with violence, rather she uses sweet talking, seduction and kindness. She is akin to the ideal witch that has chosen the salty waters as her dominion, rather than a siren or mermaid. She is an expert in healing emotional scars and matters of the heart and her way is often to induce great insight and mastery through dreams and visions. Her insight into the corrupted ways of the human mind makes her an excellent doctor of the psyche and a great instigator of obsession and insanity. She is deeply related to the seven seas and to the seven stars, as well as the rays of Venus in the moment they hit the surface of the ocean at twilight. Her numbers are three and seven and her colours are red, black and blue. She prefers dark blue or black candles in threes and sevens, with one white added.

Pontos Cantados for Pomba Gira da Praia

Pomba Gira da Praia,	*Pomba Gira of the Ocean shore,*
É uma linda Mulher,	*She is a beautiful woman,*
Ela é bonita,	*She is astonishing,*
Ela gosta do prazer.	*She adores pleasure.*

·

Na marola do Mar,	*By the tides of the sea,*
Já vem rolando,	*Look what it is bringing,*
Pomba Gira da Praia,	*Pomba Gira of the Ocean shore,*
Já deu sua risada.	*Now she gave her smile,*
Ela é Mulher bonita,	*She is a beautiful woman,*
Muito formosa,	*Very beautiful indeed,*
Trabalhando na Areia,	*Working in the sand,*
Na Encruzilhada.	*At the crossroad.*

·

Oi kererê, kererê,	*Oi kererê, kererê,*
Pomba Gira da Praia,	*Pomba Gira of the Ocean shore,*
No meio da Areia,	*In the middle of the sand,*
No meio da Praia.	*In the middle of the beach.*

Ponto Riscado of Pomba Gira da Praia
to be used when bringing down her powers

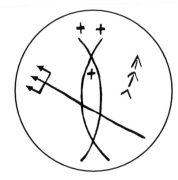

Ponto riscado of Pomba Gira da Praia
used in works of domination and seduction

A Working to calm down a man

Perform this working at the shore of the ocean dressed in white on a
Monday night. You will need to bring seven black candles, seven red
and three blue, seven cigarettes, a pair of earrings, three bracelets,
three lipsticks, a pair of clogs, matches, honey and 21 red roses. Upon
reaching the shore go into the water and wash your head, heart and

genitals, state your request to the powers of the ocean and salt waters and ask them to help you. Find a place close to the shore where you can set up the various items in a circular fashion. The items will be placed in the sand and the candles and ribbons will together with the cigarettes be placed around the clog, earring, lipsticks and bracelets. Sing a ponto for her and return to the ocean with fourteen of the roses. Follow the waves out and drop one rose just before the wave returns to the shore saying: *Tonight NN you will be calm, very calm*, with each rose. When this is finished you will go in front of the despacho and thank Pomba Gira for her help. Take seven steps backwards, turn around and go home.

When you get home write the name of the person you want to calm down on seven pieces of paper and put them in a pan. Pour sugar and honey over them and let it slowly boil whilst praying to Pomba Gira to calm him down. When it reaches a boil take it off the heat and let it cool down.

· Pomba Gira Cigana ·

These Pomba Giras are not necessarily queens, but are adopted from the sorcerous legacy of Cain and are nomadic spirits, unpredictable, helpful and demanding. Excellent fortunetellers, they can divine in any medium. She will always reveal the method of divination to her adherents, and if they follow her advice they will certainly become experts in the tool she provides them with, whether cards, shells, tea-leaves, fire or water. These Pomba Giras have been associated with the powers of Mara, which are a more accurate association than the syncretism done in the case of many other Pomba Giras. These Pomba Giras are often related to the Zingari gypsies and the kingdom of the Lyre. This kingdom contains all kinds of powers related to a bohemian lifestyle and hard tricky living, music, poetry and such. The spirits of this kingdom are therefore marked by a tendency to take chances, being fond of gambling and partying. These highly seductive Pomba Giras are the daughters of Cain and are not easily restricted.

The Ciganas can of course be found in other kingdoms, but are naturally well placed in this realm. A Cigana from the river means that her force is better cultivated in this natural location. Offerings to these spirits are usually made at the side of the road (recalling their nomadic history) or outside small lively bars and houses of pleasure. She is apt at resolving issues related to court cases and bureaucracies. She can be a great source for rejuvenating happiness, health and wealth when one has experienced losses. She can also be effective in speeding up and easing difficult divorces, especially when they have entered the legal realm.

The typical gypsy is free, independent and avoids being tied down by convention and restriction, and it is naturally enough this power the Ciganas have. She delights in fine jewelry and sweet drinks and when she comes down she shamelessly reveals the secrets of the people attending and often displays them publically in order that those present lose the shame of their faults and weaknesses. The Ciganas teach that being human comes with a dark side which should be acknowledged, celebrated and used constructively. The Pomba Gira Ciganas are many, and here are just a few of them to illustrate the serpentine and fluid nature of roads and legions when we speak of her.

Pomba Gira Cigana das Sete Saias
Pomba Gira Cigana das Almas
Pomba Gira Cigana dos Sete Cruzeiros
Pomba Gira Cigana do Pandeiro
Pomba Gira Cigana da Praça
Pomba Gira Cigana do Oriente
Pomba Gira Cigana da Lua
Pomba Gira Cigana Menina
Pomba Gira Cigana da Calunga
Pomba Gira Cigana da Rosa

Pomba Gira Cigana Zoraida
Pomba Gira Cigana Sarah
Pomba Gira Cigana Sarinha da Estrada
Maria Mulambo Cigana
Maria Padilha Cigana
Pomba Gira Cigana da Praia
Pomba Gira Cigana de Fé
Pomba Gira Cigana Maria
Pomba Gira Cigana Sulemi
Pomba Gira Cigana do Baralho
Pomba Gira Cigana da Estrela
Pomba Gira Cigana do Cabaré
Pomba Gira Cigana do Acampamento
Pomba Gira Cigana do Forno
Pomba Gira Cigana dos Infernos
Pomba Gira Cigana das Matas
Pomba Gira Cigana Sete Encruzas

Pontos Cantados for Pomba Gira Cigana

Eu bem que te avisei,	*I better warn you,*
Pra você não jogar essa cartada comigo!	*So you do not throw this card at me!*
Você apostou no valete e eu apostei nessa dama!	*You bet on the Knight but I bet on this Dame!*
Amigo você não me engana!	*Buddy, you can't cheat me!*
Vamos saravar pomba-gira Cigana.	*Let us greet Gypsy Pomba Gira.*

.

Vinha caminhando a pé,   I came here by foot,
Para ver se encontrava Pomba-Gira   To meet Gypsy Pomba Gira!
Cigana de fé! (×2)   (×2)
Ela parou e leu minha mão,   She stopped and took my hand,
E disse-me toda a verdade,   And told me all truths,
Eu só queria saber onde mora,   I Just wanted to know where she lives
Pomba-Gira Cigana de fé.   Gypsy Pomba Gira of faith.

·

Ela é uma cigana faceira, ela é,   She is a coquettish gypsy, she is,
Ela é das sete linhas,   She is the seven lines,
E não é do candomblé,   And it is not Candomblé,
Ela vem de muito longe,   She came from far away,
Os seus filhos ajudar,   To help her children,
Ela vem de muito longe,   She came from far away,
Saravar neste congá.   Greet this spirit from Congo.

·

No caminho do terreiro eu,   On the way to the terreiro I,
Encontrei uma mulher,   Met a woman,
Vinha linda e perfumada,   All beautiful and perfumed,
Eu quis saber quem ela é,   I wanted to know who she was,
Pomba Gira Cigana,   Gypsy Pomba Gira,
Pomba Gira, ela é,   Pomba Gira she is,
Ela vem caminhando,   She comes walking,
Ela chega girando,   She comes swirling,
Na ponta do pé. (×2)   On the tips of her toes. (×2)

Ponto Riscado for Pomba Gira Cigana

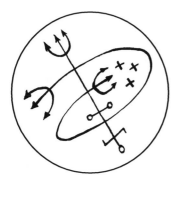

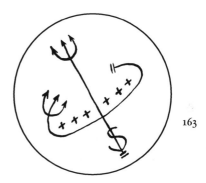

Ponto Riscado of Pomba Gira Cigana
to call upon her

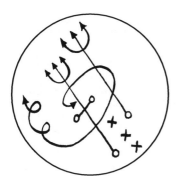

Ponto Riscado of Pomba Gira Cigana to be used in workings
when one is in the need of a fast change in a situation

A Working with Pomba Gira Cigana to tie a man to you forever

This working will be done at the crossroad on a Friday night, with the waxing moon. You will need a pair of clogs, a pair of earrings, one lipstick, seven red candles, one bottle of champagne and one of cachaça, seven red roses (without thorns), seven red ribbons and one terracotta plate. Ask permission from the powers of the crossroad and light the candles. Place the plate at the crossroad, on it mark her ponto and then place on it the clogs, earrings and lipstick together with the champagne and roses. Note that they need to be good quality items as Cigana tends to be more descriminating about the quality than most other Pomba Giras. Sing or chant her ponto and pray to her while taking small sips of the cachaça: *Pomba Gira Cigana, please come and take these your offerings, and give to me NN with love and passion now and forever more.* Recite this seven times and pour the cachaça out around the ebó, take seven steps backwards and leave the crossroad.

164

After this work, abstain completely from any sexual activity for preferably seven days, or at the least three days. On the seventh day, either with a partner or by yourself, release the sexual energies that you have stored up, preferably at midnight. Visualise vividly how this release of lust is transferred to your object of desire. But, a word of warning is required here: be careful what you wish for, especially in terms of love and bindings. I often advise people obsessed with their object of desire to read Mrabet's *Love with a Few Hairs*, and then consider whether they really want to make a hard and permanent binding.

Maria Mulambo is a beloved Pomba Gira, a patron of the poor and of widows. She is associated with the succubus Aluca which is yet again a strike in the wrong direction. Rather, the legend of Mulambo, a word which means rag, is closer to a hagiography. More a saint than a succubus. Her story goes like this:

Once upon a time there was a woman named Maria Rosa who was of low aristocratic birth, beautiful of face and kind of heart. The son of the king fell in love with Maria Rosa and when she turned fifteen a marriage was arranged. The prince was devoutly in love with her, but the love was one-sided, for Maria Rosa was in love with a poor man whom she had met in one of the poor quarters of the town. The years passed and any attempt at begetting a child failed. The prince saw her as a cherry tree that could not bear fruit. This bothered the royal family more than Maria, who invested more and more time helping the poor and needy. As the difficulties escalated at the castle, given her failure to conceive, she started to nurture the relationship with her true love. Meanwhile the king died and the prince was crowned – Maria became queen. She was much loved by the people, but also envied. Some of the aristocracy questioned her inability to beget an heir. Though the poor people whom she had helped over the years had little to give to their beloved queen, they made a carpet of flowers so she could walk upon a bed of flowers after the coronation. When the king saw how his wife was overwhelmed by love at this gesture, he was flooded with envy. When the ceremonies were over and they retired to their rooms, he beat her badly. Abuse became a common element in Maria Rosa's life. But the bruises and pain did not stop her charity, and finally the love between Maria Rosa and the poor man was consumated and she became pregnant. Maria abdicated her position in order to stay with her beloved. She took with her costly jewels and dresses, but she dressed herself in rags, like the people she loved and helped. She was finally happy in her humble condition. However, the news about Maria's pregnancy reached the king and he went insane with this knowledge, for this demonstrated that the barren tree was him. He set out to find Maria, and upon discovering her he tied stones to her body and threw her into the river. Maria sank and her tears mixed with the waters. This was done in secrecy, the people did not know about the murder. Seven days later, strange and beautiful flowers started to blossom at the riverside where the murder had taken place and the fishes went to this place and left the rest of the river empty. On this seventh day after Maria's murder her lover was drawn to this place, guided by voices from beyond. He jumped into the river and on the river bed came upon the body of his beloved. Her body was perfectly intact and she seemed more asleep than dead. He brought her back to the village and adorned her body with fine cloth and jewels. At this news, the king went crazy and remained in a delirium until his death. Her lover remained passionately in love with Maria for the rest of his life and remained without lover, wife or consort, because his Maria came to him at night comforting him and speaking with him.

Naturally, this Pomba Gira is very generous and it is difficult to cross her. Only a profound lack of understanding for one's own situation, as well as a reluctance to change, can cross her. The unfair treatment of women and widows also crosses her. Maria Mulambo is a spirit that questions what we need in order to be happy and if we are following our heart. If we do not listen to our heart we will not be able to connect with this spirit. She is a spirit that when approached comforts the one that is suffering from abuse or a loveless relationship. She can be employed to solve these situations. She usually works more slowly than other Pomba Giras and one should calculate one lunar cycle for the work to reach fruition. As this spirit is related to charity and kindness, her votaries need to express the same qualities. She is a very good remedy against depression and hopelessness.

In common with the other Pomba Giras, she likes jewels, flowers, fine wine and so on, but her demands are simple and she prefers gifts from the heart over expensive presents. Flowers that you pick yourself and give her as an offering tend to have a very beneficial effect on works done with her. It is also good to use both red cloth and a piece of rag when presenting offerings to her. Homemade sweet wine is a better offering to her than expensive champagne.

Pontos Cantados for Maria Mulambo

Mulambo Rainha Divina,	*Mulambo, divine Queen,*
A Deusa Encantada,	*Enchanted Goddess,*
Tem no seu gongar a segurança,	*She has what sounds your safety,*
Ela vem pela estrada de prata,	*She comes through the silver road,*
E caminhou num tapete de flores,	*And paths covered with flowers,*
E nem se quer se importou,	*And didn't even care,*
Ela deixou os seus súditos chorando,	*She leaves her subjects crying,*
E foi viver, no mundo da perdição,	*And left to live in the world of perdition,*
Ela deixou os seus suditos chorando,	*She left her subjects crying,*
E foi viver, no mundo da perdição,	*And left to live in the world of perdition,*

Ela è Rainha ela è mulher,	*She is Queen, she is Woman,*
Ela è Rainha ela è mulher,	*She is Queen, she is Woman,*
Pedaçinho de Mulambo para quem tem fé.	*Bits and pieces of Mulambo for the one with faith.*
É hora, é hora, calunga lhe chama,	*It is time, it is time, calunga is calling,*
É hora, é hora Mulambo vai embora. (×2)	*It is time forMulambo to leave. (×2)*
Se pedir que eu mate eu mato,	*If you ask me to kill, I will,*
Se pedir que eu dê eu dô,	*If you ask me to give pain, I will give pain,*
Se pedir que eu lhe defenda,	*If you ask that I defend,*
Eu serei seu defensor.	*I will be your defender.*

·

Meu batom é vermelho,   *My liptick is red,*
Meu coração também.   *My heart as well.*
Eu sou Maria Mulambo,   *I am Maria Mulambo,*
Como eu te quero bem.   *How I wish you well.*

·

Maria Mulambo da Encruzilhada   *Maria Mulambo of the Crossroad*
A sua saia é Mulambê...   *Your skirt is Mulambê...*
Ela é Mulambê, Ela é Mulambê.   *She is Mulambê.*

·

Pomba Gira Maria Mulambo   *Pomba Gira Maria Mulambo*
Olha minha gente, olha minha gente,   *Look my people, look my people,*
Ela é farrapo só, ela é farrapo só.   *She is just rags, just rags,*
É Pomba Gira Maria Mulambo   *It is Pomba Gira Maria Mulambo,*
É de coró, có, có, é de coró, có, co.   *É de coró, có, có, é de coró, có, co.*

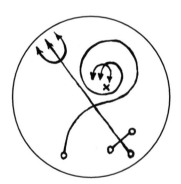

Ponto Riscado to be used in love bindings; it can also be used to attract people and open opportunities for a marriage with a wealthy man

Ponto Riscado to give strength
to Maria Mulambo

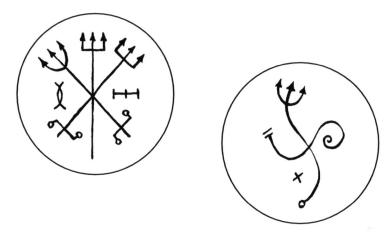

Ponto Riscado of Maria Mulambo to maximise her powers

Ponto Riscado used in works of defence and attraction; this ponto brings a
vibration similar to that of the cemetery to her powers

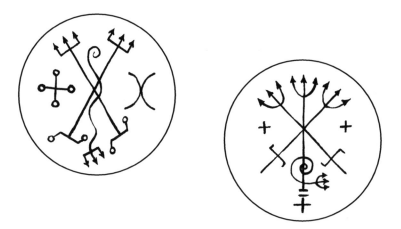

Ponto Riscado for manifesting the powers of Maria Mulambo

A Working with Pomba Gira Maria Mulambo to separate a man and his mistress

You will need:
A red cloth
Seven cigarillos
Seven red roses
One bottle of cachaça
Seven black candles
Three white candles
240 g of popcorn
250 g of cornflour
One bottle of dendê
A terracotta plate
Matches

170

Perform this working close to a dumpster, or otherwise in areas that are dirty, around midnight on a Monday or a Friday with a waning moon. Before going out, prepare the popcorn with the cornflour and dendê and place on the bottom of the plate. Take everything to a hidden place, light the candles and request license from the powers of the place you are going to use. Mark the ponto on the red cloth and place on the ground. Set the plate over the ponto and sing to Pomba Gira. Take the cigarillos and roses and roll them carefully on top of the popcorn. Place the roses aside and take up the plate and present it to your forehead, heart and genitals. Set it down again. Now take the cachaça and seven times drink a little bit and seven times spray the plate with it. Each time you spray the plate, say: *Come Pomba Gira Mulambo and help me. Separate NN from NN, his lover to such an extent that she will be a cursed mistress.* When the working is finished you will place the roses on top of the offering and leave the place.

· *Pomba Gira Sete Maridos or Pomba Gira Sete Porteiras* ·

Pomba Gira of the Seven Husbands or Seven Doors are spirits that can help in inducing firmness and stability in one's rituals. If a spirit is not responding, one can appeal to this Pomba Gira to serve as an intermediary. She is a great defence against spiritual and physical attack, and strikes down hard on anyone who is physically abusive in their relationships. She is also helpful in opening opportunities for economic growth, and providing spirit guides.

Her offerings are usually placed in front of gates and doors and her preferences and numbers are the same as with the other Pomba Giras. Her role, being married to seven Exus, leads to her being efficient in working as an intermediary between the powerful Exus, and can as such be used in order to fortify any other specific power as her domain is related to opening opportunities and doors of possibility.

It should also be mentioned that this Pomba Gira must be pampered 171 when worked with, as she is thirsty for blood and is very possessive over her votaries. She is intriguing, enigmatic and wonderful in her elegant rudeness.

Pontos Cantados for Pomba Gira da Porteira

Meu caminho é de fogo,	*My path is of the fire,*
Na porteira eu só deixo entrar,	*Through this gate you enter only if I permit,*
Quem primeiro me agradar.	*Whomever is first to please me.*
Sou Pomba Gira da Porteira.	*I am Pomba Gira of the Door.*
Levo o que tem pra levar. (×2)	*Bring to me whatever you have to give.* (×2)

·

O gira formosa tem alegria e rosa,	*The swirling one has joy and roses,*
O gira formosa tem alegria e rosa,	*The swirling one has joy and roses,*
Na gira de Pomba Gira você vem balançar,	*In the dance of Pomba Gira you will balance,*
Abre a porta da fazenda,	*Open the doors to the farm,*
E vem logo trabalhar,	*Come soon to work,*
E seus filhos saravar.	*So your children can greet you.*

·

Eu sou Pomba Gira da Porteira,	*I am Pomba Gira of the Door,*
Em cada uma tenho uma morada,	*And every one has a residence,*
Eu quero filho pra defender,	*I want children to defend,*
E inimigo pra espetar,	*And enemies to impale,*
Eu sou Pomba Gira da Porteira,	*I am Pomba Gira of the Door,*
É lá que eu faço minha morada.	*And I will make you my residency.*

Ponto Riscado of Pomba Gira da Porteira

Ponto Riscado of Pomba Gira da Porteira
to be used in works of protection

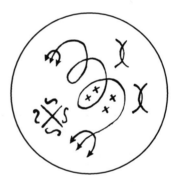

This Pomba Gira controls the affairs of the cemetery and the interaction of the dead with the living. She is at times associated with
Lamastu, which is a quite useful association. Lamastu is yet again a
vampire, but these kinds of vampires are associated with luxury and
good taste, being both seductive and deadly, much like the vibration
of this Pomba Gira. She is said to walk with Exu Veludo, an Exu that
is a fierce protector of women and a true gentleman amongst the Exus
with a taste for fine clothes, silk and fine wines. The Rainha of the
Calunga, on the other hand, work under close supervision of Omolu
and are less refined and deadlier than the Pomba Giras under her command. She is treated with ambiguity and many people have at times
mixed feeling about her. They know she can help where breaking a
couple up is desired, and she can break any kind of curse, but she is
174 demanding and must have a fondness for the person who calls her.
One needs to call her with great seriousness and even greater respect.

Her preferences are as with the other Pomba Giras but she also
takes the colour yellow. One needs to make sure that anis in one form
or another is always present when working with her. As her domain is
the cemetery, the workings are better done here or at least left in the
cemetery in the great hour so she can access her offerings directly and
work swiftly.

Pontos Cantados for Pomba Gira da Calunga

Dentro da Calunga eu vi,	*Through the Calunga I saw,*
Uma linda mulher gargalhar, (bis)	*A beautiful woman laughing,* (× 2)
Era Pomba Gira da Calunga,	*It was Pomba Gira Calunga,*
Que começava a trabalhar. (bis)	*That started to work.* (× 2)

·

Pomba Gira da Calunga,   Pomba Gira Calunga,
Nao é mulher de ninguém,   Is no one's woman,
Nao é mulher de ninguém,   Is no one's woman.
Quando entra na demanda,   When she enters the spell craft,
Só sai por sete vinténs,   She only leaves for seven pennies,
Sò sai por sete vinténs.   She only leaves for seven pennies.

•

Eu sou Pomba Gira da Calunga,   I am Pomba Gira Calunga,
E vim pra trabalhar,   I came to work,
Sou mulher de Exu Veludo,   I am the wife of Exu Veludo (Velvet),
E todo mal vou levar.   All evil I will take away.
Eu tenho una rainha,   I have a Queen,
E tenho também um rei,   I have also a King,
Obedeço a Exu Veludo,   Obedient to Exu Veludo,
Pois é ordem de meu rei.   By orders of my King.

175

•

Eu vi atravessando,   I saw on the other side,
Aquela rua,   Of that street,
Uma moça bonita,   A beautiful girl,
Vestidinha de chita (×2)   Wearing an ornamented
   cotton dress, (×2)

Mas ela era a,   But she was the,
Pomba Gira da Calunga,   Pomba Gira Calunga,
Que arrebentou,   Who took control over,
Sete catacumbas. (×2)   Seven catacombs. (×2)

Ponto Riscado of Pomba Gira da Calunga
used to call upon this power

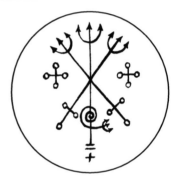

Ponto Riscado of Pomba Gira da Calunga that can be used both in works of
attraction and works that needs a stabilising element

A gift to Calunga so her support is with you

This is a simple working with many benefits. You will need:
A bottle of cachaça
A bottle of champagne
A bottle of dendé
Pork meat
A wooden tray
A virgin chalice
Seven red candles
Seven white candles
A black cloth
A white cloth
Tostão
Cigarettes
Cigar

Begin your working by honoring the gates of the cemetery in the ways explained in the section on Sete Encruzilhadas. Bring with you a virgin tray, dendé, a boneless piece of peppered raw pork (meaning, you will fry it for a few second on each side in dendé), seven roses and a bottle of cachaça and one of champagne. Then go either to the Cruzeiro or to a sepulchre you have worked with before and here ask permission to make your offerings. Place a white and black cloth on the ground and the tray with the pork upon it. Call her as you light seven white and seven red candles. Light seven cigarettes and place around the cloth, together with the candles. Sing to her and pour the dendé over the dish and then the cachaça. Pour champagne in the glass, let it spill over and pour the rest on the ground around the chalice. Spend some time in vigil, then leave by taking three steps backwards. Greet the guardian of the gate on the way out and make sure you expel hostile spirits from you before you enter your home. This is easily done with water and salt. This working is a general base for spellcraft and demands can be made upon presenting this offering. It is also good to give these gifts solely to give support to one's relationship with the spirits.

Maria Quitéria is surrounded by many tales of how she came into being. All of them reflect the same independent type of woman as Maria Padilha. Most of the legends relate this Pomba Gira to guerilla movements, both in Spain and Brazil. She is also related to Maria Bonita, the wife of the Robin Hood style villain Lampião who roamed all over Brazil and especially in the north east of the country. She works in the kingdom of the Lyre and is closely related to Maria Padilha. This powerful Pomba Gira is also found in other kingdoms, as she is associated more with a type of woman, one who will find her place in any environment. Given her relation to guerilla movements, she is also associated with assassins as well as loyalty to a cause and her adherents. She is symbolised by the dagger, which is always close at hand, and with maturity. She is extremely effective when used in works of attack 178 and to sow discord and insecurity behind enemy lines. She is deeply related to forces such as Iansan and Oba and works well side by side with Ogum, the maioral and Omolu. She is associated with Lamia, a succubus that rose to prominence in the romantic era.

Her preferences are the same as the other Pomba Giras and she is worked well anywhere, but especially in the woods and at T-junctions.

Pontos Cantados Of Maria Quitéria

Maria Quitéria,	*Maria Quitéria,*
Se ela é das Almas,	*She is of the Souls,*
No Cemitério...	*In the Cemetery...*
Vence demandas.	*Victorious in all requests.*

·

Tem faca, faca, faca,	*She has a knife, knife, knife,*
Maleva não é!	*She is not bad!*
Tem faca, faca, faca,	*She has a knife, knife, knife,*
Padilha não é!	*Padilha she is not!*
É Maria Quitéria,	*It is Maria Quitéria,*
é Maria Quitéria,	*it is Maria Quitéria,*
É Maria Quitéria,	*It is Maria Quitéria,*
é Maria Quitéria!	*it is Maria Quitéria!*

·

Ali vem sá Maria Quitéria	*Here comes Maria Quetéria,*
Trazendo um axé no pé,	*Bringing Power around her feet,*
Balançando a sua saia,	*Balancing with her skirt,*
Reforçando a nossa fé.	*Enhances our faith.*

Existe um Exu-Mulher,	*There is an Exu Woman,*
Que não passeia à toa,	*Who does not walk a tight rope,*
Quando passa pela encruza,	*When she passed through the crossing,*
Maria Quitéria não vacila,	*Maria Quitéria never falters,*
Ela não faz coisa boa.	*She does not do good things.*

·

Eu vi num cruzeiro uma mulher,	*I saw at the cross a woman,*
Vestida de branco e preto,	*Dressed in White and black,*
Dando gargalhadas ao luar,	*Laughing at the moon,*
Ela era Maria Quitéria,	*She was Maria Quitéria,*
Que chegou para trabalhar.	*Who came to work.*
Quá, quá, quá, Quitéria,	*Quá, quá, quá, Quitéria,*
Que bonito povo arreia,	*How beautiful the people of the sand,*
Que linda é sua falange,	*How beautiful your legions,*
Que bonita é Maria Quitéria.	*How beautiful Maria Quitéria.*

Ponto Riscado for Maria Quitéria, used to bring down her powers
and in personal mediumistic activity with this Pomba Gira

This Pomba Gira is properly enough related to Nagini, a serpentine goddess of the Kaula Tantrikas, and work within the domains of poisons, potions and seduction. She is an extremely dangerous Pomba Gira and it is imperative that one enters into a close and personal relationship with her if one intends to use her. She represents more of a principle, and is less related to the world of kiumbas and dead spirits. She is rarely chosen to do works, but serves better as a familiar or an advisor. She is said to preserve the mysteries of the transmission of wisdom which occured when the forbidden fruit was eaten in the Garden of Eden, and is said to have been the genii that inspired the transgression of Cheva (Eve) into the pulsating realm of godhood.

She is related to the kingdom of Crossroads where she accepts offerings of snake and scorpion, both alive and dried. Her *assentamento* needs to be constructed upon the foundation of a serpent's egg and opals, supervised by Exu das Matas and the caboclos. She is also a teacher in the art of sexual magic where she often chooses as her companion Exu Morcego. She speaks and acts quite differently from other Pomba Giras, and her powers can be sustained by Dan, Danbalah and Osumaré. In her expression she may remind us of the Voudon Lwa Shili bo Nouvavou. Her colours are green, red and black and she likes cachaça mixed with honey or cinnamon.

181

The Pomba Gira Dama da Noite is associated with the flowering and sweet smelling tree of the same name (*cestrum nocturnum*). She works in the kingdom of the Lyre and is a Pomba Gira from the cabaret and houses of pleasure and entertainment, like Geishas who as trained professionals would entertain tired soldiers after battle.

She is an erotic and sensual Pomba Gira, usually depicted in a simple black dress. She is a Pomba Gira well suited to helping people that work in the entertainment business and especially women facing problems of respect in their occupation or life. Matters such as fathers neglecting their duties to their children and harassment from colleagues can be solved by appealing to this Pomba Gira. She can help women to overcome shyness and get in touch with themselves.

Her presence is gentle and sweet, she is a Pomba Gira that never reveals secrets but can be a good ally. She understands her adherent's needs and provides solutions that are beneficial to personal growth. She is also a Pomba Gira related to the sexual mysteries of Quimbanda and can be appealed to through mystical love making.

Her preferences are the same as with the other Pomba Giras, but with a specific taste for fine champagne and sweet nut liquors. She can be found around bars, places of amusement and entertainment, T-junctions, and in the erotic depths of night. Her assentamento is often made inside bamboo where creeping plants have decided to wind their way in a beautiful decoration around her secret. She is an important Pomba Gira for the manufacture of specific oils of attraction.

Ponto Cantado for Pomba Gira Dama da Noite

Ela veio no clarão da lua,	*She comes in the fullness of the moon,*
Dama da Noite a gira é sua.	*Lady of the night, the party is yours.*
Ela é Pomba Gira de fé,	*She is Pomba Gira of faith,*
Que trabalha de acordo	*Who works in agreement*
com a maré.	*with the tide.*
Deu meia noite ela	*In the middle of the night*
deu sua risada,	*she smiles at you,*
Saravá Dama da Noite,	*Greetings lady of the Night,*
Rainha da madrugada.	*Queen of the darkest night.*

Ponto Riscado for Pomba Gira Dama da Noite

This Pomba Gira is very stern and demanding. Make sure that any request made to her is motivated by just causes before agreeing to do work with her. If a person appeals to her with requests she finds dubious, she tends to agree either to effectuate the work in a way that brings hard lessons to that person, or she will refuse to speak with them, taking the request as an insult. She enjoys rigour and discipline; those who come to her for aid need to demonstrate these qualities as well as integrity if they wish to inspire her benevolence and willing-ness to help. She is syncretised with beings like the Rusalki which is a quite useful association, but alas, this class of night flying witch-vampires are often misunderstood. As with the other Pomba Giras, she is very sensual but her sensualism has the power of inducing respect and not sensual appetite.

184   She can be called upon at T-junctions as well as crossroads and in the cemetery. She resolves problems of fertility and helps families that are about to break up to find their way back together again. Her preferences are the same as the other Pomba Giras.

Ponto Riscado for Pomba Gira Rainha das Almas

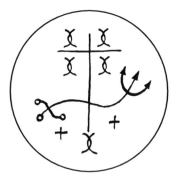

Ponto Cantado for Pomba Gira das Almas

> *Pomba Gira das Almas vem tomar*   Pomba Gira of the souls come to take
> *chô chô,*   cho chô,
>
> *Pomba Gira das Almas vem tomar*   Pomba Gira of the souls come to take
> *chô chô,*   chô chô.
>
> *Vencedora de demandas vem tomar*   The victorious one comes to take
> *chô chô,*   chô chô,
>
> *Vencedora de demandas vem tomar*   The victorious one comes to take
> *chô chô.*   chô chô.[†]

† This term *chô chô* is used to cover foul words used when designating great havoc.

· *Pomba Gira da Luar* ·

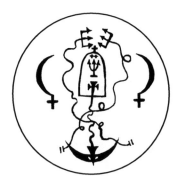

The Pomba Gira of the lunar rays is another very mysterious Pomba Gira that works within the erotic realm and is best utilised as an advisor. She is sometimes associated with the Polish class of vampires known as Upierzyca. These vampires fit with the classic idea of vampires as beautiful and lusting females sleeping in tombs by day and

attacking their prey by night. She is also related to the *loup garou* or shape shifting witches, that become animals in their night flights. She is intimately related to the mysteries of Quimbanda and the secrets of activating the darker and the more vile forces of nature. She ties in, as does Pomba Gira das Cobras, whose arcana remains largely undisclosed in Quimbanda, with the true meaning of the vampire secrets. These are far from the vulgar and popular image one can glean from movies and books, with the exception of Bram Stoker's work.

· Pomba Gira Menina ·

Pomba Gira Menina is the consort of Exu Mirim and as her name suggests is a young Pomba Gira who represents the energy and challenges of youth. It is difficult to isolate any coherent history of this Pomba Gira as the stories and legends are so many and varied. This Pomba Gira dwells in places where young people like to meet, especially where dance, drinking and clandestine activities are carried out. She can be called upon in gardens and at the roadside, which links her to the Ciganas at some level. She can be approached in difficult cases where the other Pomba Giras fail to manifest the request, as she tends to find a route through any predicament.

She thrives on obsession, compulsion and secrets, and probes deep into the human psyche and soul. Those who work with her must be prepared to deal with their own darker strains as a part of the process. If she finds a person to her liking she helps this person with an amazing passion and is well suited to finding true love and not the temporary relationships of sensual pleasure which tend to be the case when one asks Pomba Gira to manifest a partner.

She also works well with Exu Tranca Ruas and is said to manifest like a laughing angel. She likes cider, soft alcoholic and sweet drinks and she also accepts yellow roses.

Pontos Cantados of Pomba Gira Menina

Olha que menina,	*Look, what a girl,*
Olha que menina bela,	*Look what a beautiful girl,*
É Pomba Gira menina,	*It is Pomba Gira girl,*
Me chamando na anela.	*She is called to the circle.*

·

Ciganinha, ciganinha,	*Little gypsy, little gypsy,*
Da sandália de pau (×2)	*Wearing sandals of wood,* (×2)
Quando ela bate o pé,	*When she stamps her foot*
Ela faz o bem,	*She makes things good,*
E não faz o mal.	*She does not make things bad.*

Ponto Riscado of Pomba Gira Menina used in works of attraction & amorous conquest. It can also be used as a basis for building her assentamento

Ponto Riscado of Pomba Gira Menina

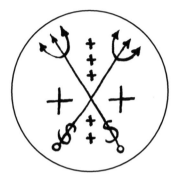

*Ponto Riscado used in more ritual circumſtances, & whiĉ can also be used in
personal mediumiſtic workings for eſtablishing contaĉt with her*

190   This Pomba Gira is yet another mysterious spirit, said to be associated with the demons of storms called Keteb. This word is from the Hebrew meaning destruction and is associated with famine, storms and annihilation of a supernatural kind, reputed to bring about destruction at noon. She manifests with the horns of a goat and with dark wings. She takes her nutrition from thunder and lightning and is manifested in the wind. She is also related to Schemesh, in his aspect as Lord of the Sun in the Kingdom of Death. This means that she is the presence of the sun as it shines upon the dead. Her mysteries are deep and mainly undisclosed. She is related more to natural phenomena and represents a specific body of wisdom which is different and less workable that many other Pomba Giras. Her colours are black and dark yellow and she works directly under Lucifer. She is deeply related to the mysteries of Quimbanda, or the *animated skull*, and should be treated with great care and respect.

Pomba Gira Rosa Caveira is said to have a double face. One side is beautiful, but the other is that of a skull. As such both her character and appearance is reproduced in Casey's *Lucifer* under the guise of Mazikeen. She belongs to the kingdom of Souls and lives in the cemetery where she works closely with Tata Caveira and Exu Caveira.

There are many myths about her that place her both in Mongolia some 2500 before the birth of Christ, contemporaneous with Christ, and also in Spain and Italy in the 15th and 16th century. The various myths are similar in spite of their geographical variations. The story tells of a family, rich in land and with seven daughters. The mother had a passion for roses and the name Rose was given to all the daughters. But with the birth of the seventh daughter the mother died and the girl received the name Rosa Caveira, Rose of the Skull. The mother, who was a powerful sorceress, passed on her amazing powers to Rosa Caveira by dying in childbirth. The father resented this last daughter because of the mother's death and she was raised by her grandparents. The mother's grave was prepared in the house the family was living in and Rosa Caveira grew up guided by her mother's spirit who taught her how to use her powers. The family had a tradition of helping people in need and so Rosa Caveira followed suit and in doing so became an object of envy for her sisters. An alternative version of the story is that the mother was helping in childbirth when the patient died and the child survived, and thus received the name Rosa Caveira and the infusion of witch power came from the midwife. In any case, Rosa Caveira was blessed with immense powers, a great sensitivity and tremendous mediumistic abilities. The father also took a special interest in Rosa Caveira and taught her the art of the warrior and the use of swords and knives, whilst the spirit of the mother instructed her in the work of potions and magic. The jealousy of the sisters grew until they accused Rosa Caveira of being a daughter of the devil, claiming that her knowledge came from demons. Rosa Caveira's beauty did not help the situation. When Rosa Caveira was 19 her oldest sister got married to a rich man and she attempted to take her life. This angered Rosa Caveira and she caused her sister's death. This led to her being abandoned by her family and she left her village to see the world. She encountered a 77 year old wizard in her wanderings who made her his apprentice and taught her in the cemetery. This man taught Rosa Caveira how to work Quimbanda, and by this we mean the black arts of Quimbanda: how to work the animated skull and the secrets of necromancy. But her sisters had not forgotten about her and conspired to kill her. For this they hired another wizard who, with slyness and using the powers of roses, managed to kill Rosa Caveira and imprison her spirit. Rosa Caveira's teacher came to her aid and freed the spirit so she could seek out her deserved revenge upon her family and the wizard who imprisoned her. The wizard that used to be Rosa Caveira's teacher passed her legacy on to his students and her renown was spread to all the corners of the world.

As can be seen from the legend, she is a powerful spirit well suited both as a teacher and as an avenger. She is expert in turning enemies into slaves and attacks with the cold fury that is characteristic of Tatá Caveira and Exu Caveira who are her companions. She hates traitors and deceivers, she is the very image of the witch and warrior meeting in perfect synthesis. She is quite obscure and is careful in her dealings with others, but tends to bond very affectionately with her chosen ones. She is said by some to enter at the hinges of the door, which

gives her an association with Cranea, the mercurial nymph, servant of Hecate who lives at the hinges and in the cherry tree, a favored fruit for all Pomba Giras, and in particular Rosa Caveira.

She is better worked on Mondays and Fridays and she takes the colours black, red and yellow. Her preferences are like the other Pomba Giras, but she also has a liking for knives and various types of peppers, especially malangueta.

Ponto Cantado for Pomba Gira Rosa Caveira

Rosa Caveira ... Rosa Caveira...	*Rose Skull... Rose Skull...*
Ela é o Exu que nasceu na porteira!	*She is the Exu that was Born at the door!*
Não se põe sobre a mata,	*Don't place out in the woods,*
Não se põe sobre a mesa,	*Don't take away from the table,*
Ela é o Exu que acompanha o Caveira!	*She is the Exu Who walks with Caveira!*

· *Pomba Gira de Angola* ·

This Pomba Gira is also known as Rainha de Candomblé and is the Pomba Gira that serves as an intermediary and point of reference between various orixa and minkisi as they are mirrored within the legions of Exu and Pomba Gira. It is her mystery that made it possible for Exu and Pomba Gira to be a part of many forms of the Yoruba inspired religion of Candomblé. This Pomba Gira is the archetypical African woman who came with slavery to Brazil. She had to work with the few tools at hand to raise the cult of spirits and cultivated an independence and supremacy based upon the force of will and the fire of need. She represents the establishment of African faiths in Brazil, which were, after all, worked largely by the women that came to Brazil, especially in Bahia. This Pomba Gira is ruled by force and motivation, a deep determination to carry things through and is extremely knowledgeable. It is a Pomba Gira that seeks to preserve tradition and she manifests in serious forms, rarely coquettish and sensual, but more like a mature woman who has lived and thus knows and cherishes the more serious side of life and social organisation. She has the same preferences as the other Pomba Giras in terms of offerings, in particular spices, cachaça and anisette. Her day is Friday and she can be called upon in any place, but preferably at T-junctions, and also crossroads. She can serve as a wise and good guide for Mãe de Santos and is excellent in workings that demand solving social confusion, gossip and retaining order in situations that have been previously organised but are about to fall apart.

Pontos Cantados for Pomba Gira de Angola

Bateu meia noite na capela,	*The chapel struck midnight,*
O galo cantou na encruzilhada (×2)	*The cock sung at the crossroad* (×2)
Arruma tua capa e teu garfo, meu Exu,	*Take your cape and trident my Exu,*
O meu pai Ogum te chamou de madrugada,	*My father Ogum calls you in the darkest night,*
Encruza tá te chamando,	*The crossing calls you,*
Pomba Gira de Angola.	*Pomba Gira from Angola.*

•

Candongueiro, quando chama,	*Candongeiro, when calling,*
É sinal que está na hora,	*It means the time has come,*
Candongueiro, quando chama,	*Candongeiro, when calling,*
É que Exu já vai embora.	*It means Exu needs to leave.*
Pomba Gira de Angola,	*Pomba Gira de Angola,*

Amarra a saia que Exu vai embora,　*Tie up your skirt and leave,*

Pomba Gira de Angola,　*Pomba Gira from Angola,*

Amarra a saia que Exu　*Tié up your skirt, it is time for you*
tá na hora.　*and Exu to leave.*

·

Exu já curimbou, Exu jà curiou,　*Exu is singing, he has now sung,*

Exu vai embora que Ogum mandou,　*Exu takes away what Ogum tells,*

Vai com Pomba Gira de Angola,　*Came with Pomba Gira from Angola,*

Vai para longe, vai para Angola,　*Came from far away, came from Angola,*

Vai Pomba Gira que encruza já chamou,　*They are coming when the crossing is calling,*

Exu ja curiou, Exu já curimbou.　*Exu sung, Exu is singing.*

Ponto Riscado that manifests the full force of Pomba Gira de Angola and can be used in particularly strong workings

Ponto Riscado for Pomba Gira de Angola.

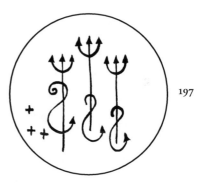

197

Ponto Riscado of Pomba Gira de Angola

A Working with Pomba Gira de Angola for making a man leave your life

This working is best done at the front of the door of the person you want to leave. Make sure that the person is at home and will not be leaving his apartment or house. If this is not possible, do it as close as possible to his house and make sure you procure a copy of the key to his door. You will need three black candles, three black and three red ribbons, seven chicken brains (or hearts), castor oil, yours and his name written on a piece of red paper, a picture of the man you want to get rid of in total, a black cloth and a virgin plate. Bring all these items to his door some minutes before midnight on a Friday or a Monday. If this cannot be done, make it as close as possible and add the key to his door to the ebo/despacho. Put the oil on the plate together with your names and cross it with the ribbons. It should be placed upon a black cloth marked with the ponto of Pomba Gira.

198 Place the picture on top of everything. Silently sing her pontos and ask her to take this man away from you, take him to the other side of the world and make him disappear from your life. You will then go home and fumigate your house and take a bath in sea salt. In the early morning hours as the sun is rising, return to the same place and pack up the ebo together in the black cloth, promise Pomba Gira that you will give her seven red roses, champagne and cigarettes when the man leaves your life. Your will dispose of the ebo by throwing it in some wild place close to where he lives.

Her story is of a young girl, sweet and soft tempered, whose mother   199
died in childbirth. Her father placed the burden of guilt for the
mother's death upon the daughter, and at the age of fourteen she was
abandoned by him when he found a new love. She took work as a
maid cleaning houses where her first boss raped her. She stayed there
for some time suffering this abuse until she decided to prostitute herself, in this way at least she would have better control over the abusers.
After some years as a prostitute she started work in a bar. Here she
was graced with kindness by a crime lord. He took care of her without
ever suggesting any debt, in fact he never revealed his name to her. He
always gave her money and small gifts so she could get by with more
ease. After a long night at work she went to her simple house, and this
particular evening she decided to take a shortcut through a back alley
where she encountered a man that was up to no good. She tried to run
in the opposite direction, but found her exit blocked by another man.
At his foot lay the corpse of her benefactor. Filled with despair she
called upon St George and was set aflame by him as the two culprits
drew closer. She grasped her razor and slashed the two men to death,
avenging her benefactor and herself. After this she left for the North-
east of Brazil and opened her own bar. She progressed rapidly and

ended her life alone but content, always being nurtured by the memories of the one good man and St George.

This story is interesting as it is represents a complete overlay of themes between the abused woman and the story of a saint.

Her colours are white, black and red. She drinks campari and martini in addition to the common preferences. She is represented by a razor floating in honey. She also has a great affinity with black swans and ducks.

Pontos Cantados for Pomba Gira Maria Navalha

Ô Navalha, ô Navalha	*Hail Razor, Hail Razor*
O seu poder não falha	*Your power does not fail*
Ô Navalha, ô Navalha	*Hail Razor, Hail Razor*
O seu poder não falha	*Your power does not fail*

·

Cabaré na Lapa. fica até de madrugada	*The Cabaret in Lapa[†] is open until dawn*
Maria Navalha espera	*Maria Navalha waits until the*
o dia clarear ... (×2)	*break of the day ... (×2)*
Já chamou Seu Tranca Ruas,	*She already called Seu [Sir] Tranca Ruas,*
Já chamou Seu Zé Pelintra Seu	*She already called Seu Zé Pelintra, Seu*
Marinheiro vem	*Marinheiro also comes*
de alto mar ... (×2)	*from the high seas ... (×2)*
É na Lapa, na Lapa espera	*It is in Lapa, in Lapa she waits until the*
o dia clarear...(×2) ...	*break of the day ... (×2)*

† Lapa, a disrict in São Paulo.

This Pomba Gira is the root of all. She is the burning bush that spoke to Moses, she is the notorious tree of fire that blazes under our feet, she is the sum of knowledge. In her, good and bad is met as one fervent radiant pyre of infinite expression. She is the power all Exus are guarding and all Pomba Giras adhere to. Some of her stories tell of a Roman noblewoman, others of a French or Spanish woman, who was born into wealth and abused it. She had no shame and took her will and fill of the pleasures of the world. It was only when her devoted husband died that she realised that she had lost her support. The sadness of this realisation set her on fire, some say a stigmata of flames, and she passed away in this state.

Interestingly, the root of Pomba Gira's fire rests in the recognition of support and equality between male and female so they can move as one. This is the fundamental message of this retinue of fire and blood, blossom so he can adore and be called to protect. She is not pronouncing a feminist gospel, but her cry is one of unity. And it is because of her that Quimbanda is so challenging. It is a spirit herd that wants us to achieve a union with the truth which we have hidden in our soul.

Pontos Cantados for Pomba Gira Rainha da Figueira do Inferno

Sua gargalhada ecoa na madrugada	Her laughter echoes in the dead of night
A Dona Figueira não é cinzas, ela é brasa	Lady Fig is not ashes, she is burning coals
O sol, a lua, louvamos com fé	We praise the sun and the moon in faith
A Dona Figueira tá pro que der e vier	Lady Fig is here for better or worse
Tá pro que der e vier (×2)	For better or worse (×2)
Não mexa com a Figueira, brincadeira ela não é	Don't mess with the Fig, she is no joke
Tá pro que der e vier (×2)	For better or worse (×2)
Não mexa com a Figueira, brincadeira ela não é	Don't mess with the Fig, she is no joke

.

Transforma espinho em rosa, se fores merecedor	She turns thorns into roses, if you're worthy
Na barra de sua saia ninguém nunca encostou	The edge of her skirt nobody shall touch
Labareda de fogo queima, é o aviso que ela dá	Flaming fire burning, is the warning that she gives
Quem quer caminhos floridos com ela não vai brincar	Anyone on the path of flowers she will never entertain
Tá pro que der e vier (×2)	For better or worse (×2)
Não mexa com a Figueira, brincadeira ela não é	Don't mess with the Lady Fig, she is no joke
Tá pro que der e vier (×2)	For better or worse (×2)
Não mexa com a Figueira, brincadeira ela não é	Don't mess with the Lady Fig, she is no joke

.

Root Ponto Cantado of Pomba Gira Rainha da Figueira do Inferno

A Pomba Gira debaixo de uma Figueira   *Pomba Gira under a Fig tree*

Ela dançava envolta de uma fogueira   *She danced around the campfire*

A Pomba Gira debaixo de uma Figueira   *Pomba Gira under a Fig tree*

Ela dançava envolta de uma fogueira   *She danced around the campfire*

A Pomba Gira deu uma   *Pomba Gira laughed*
forte gargalhada   *loudly*

Ela venceu os inimigos   *She conquered the enemies*
no meio da encruzilhada   *in the middle of the crossroads*

A Pomba Gira deu uma   *Pomba Gira laughed*
forte gargalhada   *loudly*

Ela venceu os inimigos   *She conquered the enemies*
no meio da encruzilhada   *in the middle of the crossroads*

This Pomba Gira finds her reflection in the Seven Doors, Pomba Gira of Seven Husbands. She is the seven planets but also the seven stars that mark half of the celestial Draco. Any celestial aspirations of love and eros will go through her and she will transmit this upon the Earth – or rather within it – to the Queen of the Fig Tree. These mysteries penetrate so deeply into the core of Quimbanda that they deserve a volume to themselves. For now it should suffice to say that this Pomba Gira is the velvet veil that calms the fire. She is the starry night that embraces you in comfort. She forms part of the mystery of the crowned dragon, she who owns the fiery centre of the earth and the diamond in the crown given to the Queen of the Fig Tree.

Quiet meditation upon her pontos riscados accompanied with green candles, absinthe and red wine should suffice.

205

Two Pontos for Rainha Sete Estrelhas

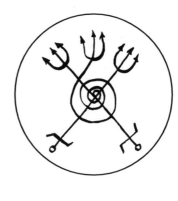

Cadenza

AND HERE ENDS THE BOOK, born under the constant outpouring of Pomba Gira Rainha da Figueria do Inferno and given to Woman, so she and her queendom can be ever vibrant in their beauty. The aim of this book has been to open the doors to a cult of many kingdoms, where Her fire is supported and mediated by her many kings and knights. This book has been monitored by spirit itself and mediated through continuous work with the queens of our house, who revealed substantial mysteries of a profound nature, pertinent to understanding the nature of the cult itself. Quimbanda is a cult of spirit reverence, and in fact both falls and rewards are gained by acknowledging this fact. We need to approach these spirits in admiration, with trust and love for them as they are, and not because of what they can do for us in terms of material transformation of our fortunes. Approach them as tutors and guides and they will open the door girdled with diamonds and bliss and not coal and difficulties. As such they present us with the choice of embracing suffering and confusion on the path of malice, or exalting this by the virtue of the spirit of understanding and thus realise all shades of power.

Quimbanda is the cult of the fig tree of fire in Hell and its reflexes upon the denizens of the land in their meeting with the stars. This book has set forth principles of the cult, many of which have been forgotten, and some held back from revelation until now. Side by side with the traditional expression of the cult the landscape has been presented in a way which enables us to work with these spirits motivated by a deeper sense of appreciation and a desire for better understanding.

To open the landscape further I want to share the story of two Pomba Giras as they manifested in contemporary women. One of them, let us call her Maria Dominatrix, was from an early age exposed to sadistic demands from her father. She suffered abuse, but married a true son of St. George. This gave her the freedom to be secure and to work upon taking back her soul. She ventured into caverns of leather and flesh where the whip sung. She took back her worth and herself in a form that made her triumph. Her success in love, work, money and joy testifies to this. We find here a woman, proud in her womanhood and sexuality, with a St George that supports her. Here we find Pomba Gira taking the throne of Hell where she lashes out because she can – she knows who she is.

Next we have the Pomba Gira manifesting in Maria de Campo, a Pomba Gira of the fields and the wild. This Pomba Gira suffered the lustful eyes of men from an early age, and on many occasions lustful elderly gentlemen were placed on her path, and she had to fight off the sordid advances of inferior beings, males in the making so to speak. She found her pleasure with the inferior, mimicking something higher in the recognition of lust. When she found love, lust took new proportions and her attention turned towards a quiet life in the embrace of the wild mountains. Here she could live the ecstasy of many with one. She too found a knight, a St George that made it his purpose in life to guard her and nurture her with love. In these two cases, which represent extremes of possible manifestations, we find self-assertive women who gravitate around the point of seductive womanhood, and the blessing of the knight that gives freedom to this marvelous unfolding. I believe woman should be supported in her freedom. Any man who is a knight will support this realisation that millennia of condemnation must find its release. We males, good knights of love, can guard and follow, but never abandon; some must take on the curses of their fathers whilst others move on in realisation. By allowing Woman to flower, we will meet our own challenges. We can choose love and follow it, or we can creep into a cave and resent it. Pomba Gira gives a gospel of love and freedom for those who know themselves and admit her into the chambers of the heart and soul.

Allow me to have been the scribe and vessel for this gift and may this book be embraced as a part of Her generous testament.

Salvé Pomba Gira Rainha!

Alguidar: Terracotta bowl

Amací: Herbal bath, but originally this was a beer based fermented herbal decoction that made part of one's baptism/initiation in the cult prior to the advancements over the last forty years.

Amarrar: To bind, most often used to refer to love spells aiming towards binding one person to another.

Arruanda: An alternative spelling of Luanda in Congo, which was a place where many slaves were shipped out in the New World. The term is used in respect of this heritage and memory.

Assentamento: The spirit vessel usually made in a terracotta jar to house the spirits.

Buraco: Literally *hole*, but a term used for people that are in a state of disgrace and poverty, a bad stage in their life.

Caboclo: Native Indian, indigenous to Brazil, but more generally used in reference to the spirits of knowledge found in the wilderness.

Cachaça: Sugar cane alcohol.

Cambono/a: An initiate who assists the medium.

Catiço: Literally *charmed one* in reference to people suddenly disappearing in nature, like the European fairy taken, people simply disappearing in the embrace of nature, speaking of a instant transition from human to spirit. Sometimes it is also used to define the spiritual calibre of Exus and Pomba Giras as *spirits of enchantment*.

Charuto: Cigar.

Demanda: To demand, in the sense of a forceful request made to the spirit.

Dendé: Palm oil.

Ebó: A Yorubá term signifying *sacrifice*, in Quimbanda used interchangeably with mironga, see *mironga* and also *despacho*.

Egun: Departed soul.

Despacho: A magical working, often involving padê which aims to send spirits on a mission and also to clean someone from impurities. Literally a spirit voyage or exorcism.

Fundanga/Fula: Gunpowder.

Gira: Ritual celebration in honour of the spirits.

Kiumba: Similar to larvæ, spirit of the dead with a fragmented personality and memory, hence no direction. Originally from the Kikongo/Kimbundu word for *skull*.

Laroyê: A salutation of the spirits of the Quimbanda but, in reality an elision of the Yoruba *Iya Ile Ayé* , meaning *I give reverence to the mothers of the earth*.

Lomba: The grave, sepulchre.

Luanda: Alternative spelling of Arruanda, see Arruanda.

Macumba: A common phrase referring to any form of spell work and demanda, but is often used in reference to Quimbanda workings.

Malandro: Typified by Zé Pelintra and refers to the people of the streets and the kingdom of the Lyre that are related to bars, taverns, gambling and bordellos. They are commonly seen as trickster spirits that are related to chance and opportunity.

Marafo: Any high proof alcoholic distillate.

Mironga: Generic term for spellcraft, from the most simple to the most elaborate that aims towards action, also called demanda, literally a demand, a forceful request.

Nkulu: Used in reference to ones spirit guides/ Exu Tatá. Originally a Kikongo term referring to ancestry, often, but not exclusively, in a more murky way.

Padê: A dish made from manioc flour or corn flour and peppers as basic ingredients that serves as food-offering when making ebó and despacho in Quimbanda.

Pataco: Money.

Patuá: Talisman, charm, power bag.

Pemba: Sacred chalk used to draw pontos riscados, see *pontos riscados*, and can also be used as a component of magical powders.

Pitú: Cigarette.

Pontos Cantados: Songs designed to praise or manifest spirits.

Pontos Riscados: The spirit signatures or designs replicating the spirit's nature used to call them into manifestation.

Preto velho: Literally *old Blacks*, the category of spirits that preserved the African wisdom, seen as calm and wise spirits who are often used to give comfort and loosen bindings and problems.

Tabaque: A ritual session involving the calling upon spirits with drums.

Tatá: Priest in the double sense of being the one that possess the secrets of his Exu and/or Pomba Gira in the form of the spirit vessel. It is also used as a reference to one's mentor both mundane and spiritual as well as the director of a Quimbanda temple.

Terreiro/Tenda: Space or place set aside for the cultivation of the spirits of Quimbanda.

Tostão: Coins, also a shorthand for the herb tostão de Oxum, which is used to secure abundance and better financial flow.

Tronco: The trunk, the foundation of a terreiro, house of Exu and Pomba Gira. It can also signify the terreiro or temple of Exu and Pomba Gira itself as well as the first assentamento that was made for the new house – as well as referring to the main spirit giving support to the Tatá.

Yayá: Female variant of tatá, see *Tatá*.

A list of Pomba Giras

Pombagira Akiesan
Pombagira Aruá
Pombagira Carangola
Pombagira da Lomba
Pombagira das Cachoeiras
Pombagira das Flores
Pombagira Detê
Pombagira do Bananal
Pombagira do Jardim
Pombagira do Oriente
Pombagira do Rio
Pombagira do Sol e da Lua
Pombagira Ganzá
Pombagira Kirombô
Pombagira Maleva
Pombagira Maria Colodina
Pombagira Moça Bonita
Pombagira Mundana
Pombagira Rosinha
Pombagira Sete Chocalhos
Pombagira Sete Cores
Pombagira Sete Estrelas
Pombagira Sete Ondas
Pomba Gira Cigana
Pomba Gira Maria Mulambo da Porteira
Pomba Gira Maria Padilha rainha do cabaré
Pomba Gira Maria Padilha
Pomba Gira Maria Padilha das Almas
Pomba Gira Maria Padilha da Encruzilhada
Pomba Gira Maria Padilha do Cruzeiro
Pomba Gira Maria Rosa

Pomba Gira Rainha
Pomba Gira Maria Molambo
Pomba Gira Rosa Caveira
Pomba Gira Rosa da Noite
Pomba Gira das Sete Encruzilhadas
Pomba Gira do Cruzeiro
Pomba Gira da Calunga
Pomba Gira Mirongueira
Pomba Gira Maria Quitéria
Pomba Gira Maria Mulambo da Estrada
Pomba Gira Rainha das Rainhas
Pomba Gira Menina
Pomba Gira Rainha Sete Encruzilhadas
Pomba Gira Rainha do Cemitério
Pomba Gira das Almas
Pomba Gira Magdalena Sofia
Pomba Gira da Praia
Pomba Gira Dama da Noite
Pomba Gira Sete Catacumbas
Pomba Gira Sete Calungas
Pomba Gira Maria Mulambo das Sete Catacumbas
Pomba Gira Maria Mulambo da sete Encruzilhadas
Pomba Gira Fiqueira do Inferno
Pomba Gira Maria Mulambo da Porta do Cemitério
Pomba Gira Cacurucaia
Pomba Gira Maria Caveira do Cemitério
Pomba Gira Maria Mulambo da Lixeira
Pomba Gira Maria Kitelja do cuzero da almas
Pomba Gira Sete Saias
Pomba Gira Rainha da Kalunga Pequena
Pomba Gira Rainha das Almas
Pomba Gira Rainha das Matas
Pomba Gira das Cobras
Pomba Gira do Luar
Pomba Gira do Sol

Bibliography

ALVA, ANTÔNIO. *Trabalhos práticos de magia Negra*. Editora Pallas: Brazil, 1985.

BAILY, CYRIL. *The Religion of Ancient Rome*. Archibald Constable & Co. Ltd: UK, 1907.

BRAGA, LOURENÇO. *Trabalhos de Umbanda ou Magia Pratica*. Bibiloteca Espiritualista: Brazil, 1956.

BRAGA, LOURENÇO. *Umbanda e Magia Branca/Quimbanda Magia Negra* (2 volumes). Editora Borsoi: Brazil, 1951.

ASTIDE, ROGER. *The African Religions of Brazil*. Johns Hopkins University Press: US, 1978.

BROWN, DIANA DEG. *Umbanda*. Columbia University Press: US, 1986.

CAPONE, STEFANIA. *A busca da Àfrica no candomblé*. Editora Pallas: Brazil, 2004.

EUFRAZIO, POMPILIO POSSERA. *Catecismo do Umbandista*. Editora Eco: Brazil, 1964.

FONTENELLE, ALUIZIO. *Exu*. Editora Aurora: Brazil, 1954.

FRISVOLD, NICHOLAJ, DE MATTOS. *Kiumbanda*. Chadezoad: Brazil, 2006.

GREY, PETER. *The Red Goddess*. Scarlet Imprint. UK, 2007.

LECOUTEUX, CLAUDE. *The Return of the Dead*. Inner Traditions: US, 2009.

LECOUTEUX, CLAUDE. *The Secret History of Vampires*. Inner Traditions: US, 2010.

LIGIÉRO, ZECA. *Malandró Divino*. Nova Era: Brazil, 2002.

MCGREGOR, PEDRO. *The Moon and Two Mountains*. Souvenir Press: UK, 1966.

MOLINA, N.A. *Na Gira dos Exu*. Editora Espirtualista: Brazil (n/d)

——. *Saravá Exu*. Editora Espiritualista: Brazil (n/d)

——. *Saravá Maria Padilha*. Editora Espiritualista: Brazil (n/d)

——. *Saravá Pomba Gira*. Editora Espiritualista: Brazil (n/d)

MOREIRA, ALDEMAR. *Formas populares da Religião*. Editora Iresi: Brazil (n/d)

SOUZA, LAURA DE MELLO. *O Diabo e a terra de Santa Cruz*. Compania das Letras: Brazil, 1987.

ST. CLAIR, DAVID. *Drum and Candle*. Mac Donald & Co: UK, 1971.

STRATTON-KENT, JAKE. *The True Grimoire*. Scarlet Imprint: UK, 2009.

TEIXEIRA, ANTÔNIO ALVES. *A Magia e os Encantos da Pomba-Gira*. Editora Eco: Brazil, 1970.

215

Made in the USA
Las Vegas, NV
20 March 2024

87509615R00134